One Aryan Nation under God

1999 Reinhold Niebuhr Minister and Scholar Award

One Aryan Nation under God

How Religious Extremists Use the Bible to Justify Their Actions

Jerome Walters

SOURCEBOOKS, INC.
NAPERVILLE, ILLINOIS

Published by Sourcebooks
P.O. Box 4410, Naperville, Illinois 60567-4410
(630) 961-3900   FAX: (630) 961-2168

First edition published 2000 by The Pilgrim Press. Hardcover edition published 2001 by Sourcebooks, Inc., by arrangement with The Pilgrim Press.

Library of Congress Cataloging-in-Publication Data

Walters, Jerome, 1964-
    One aryan nation under God: how religious extremists use the Bible
    to justify their beliefs / by Jerome Walters.
        p. cm.
Originally published: Cleveland, Ohio: Pilgrim Press, 2000.
Includes bibliographical references and index.
    ISBN 1-57071-740-0 (alk. paper)
    1. White supremacy movements—United States. 2. Christian Identity
    (Sect) 3. Racism—United States—Religious aspects—Christianity. 4.
    Radicalism—United States. 5. United States—Race relations. I. Title.

E184.A1 .W218 2001
261.8'348'00973–dc21

00-066159

Printed and bound in the United States of America
BG 10 9 8 7 6 5 4 3 2 1

To Kristi, Isaac, David, and Jessica

CONTENTS

PREFACE

T his work, which exposes and responds to an expression of racial extremism called Christian Identity and groups allied with it, has its rationale in the very giving of the gospel by God. God has made the person of God known in the birth and history of the people Israel. And God has come and lived among us in Jesus (John 1:14), who went public with the good news. Christians, in turn, are called to risk a claim in the world for God's promised coming kingdom and the sovereign loving reign of Jesus Christ. The church's shared ministry is rooted in a God who through the risen Jesus (and who actually uses the likes of us!) continues to give God's love to all within earshot, who have their hands out for the bread and wine of Holy Communion or who are washed in the waters of baptism. The drive by God is to go into the world bearing witness to the mystery hidden for ages but now revealed through the church (Eph. 3:7–12). Long before racial extremists began spreading their racial gospel, the call went out to the church to proclaim God's promises for all people. It is not that God has elected a certain race of people from the beginning and sends Jesus, and in turn other white kinsmen, to call the Aryan race out from among Jews and people of color. The Christian church's ministry is given by a God whose desire is to adopt children from "every tribe and language and people and nation" (Rev. 5:9). It is my hope that this work will contribute in some way to this ministry entrusted to the church.

This is a truly contextual work, having been cultivated and formulated on the scene, in the midst of doing ministry in Roundup, Montana. The logic of its presentation follows (I hope in a more systematic way) the logic I used in responding to expressions of racial extremism I encountered in Montana and across the country. The first chapter brings the reader along via personal experiences that escalated the need for a public voice. Following this, the chapters systematically expose today's expressions of racial extremism until, in the final chapter, a response by and for the church is ventured.

I would like to thank the members of Zion Lutheran Church in Roundup, Montana, who supported and prayed for me and the church in times of trial, and perceived my response to racial extremism, which at times took me outside Roundup, as an extension of my public ministry. I would also like to thank the congregation I last served, Bethlehem Lutheran Church, whose members, as I finished this work, surrounded and uplifted me with love and prayer. I am indebted as well to my teachers at Luther Seminary in St. Paul, to Dr. Craig Koester and David Norland for reading the manuscript and offering wisdom and encouragement, and to The Pilgrim Press and Sourcebooks, Inc. for publishing the work. Finally, I am deeply grateful for my family, whose love, patience, and support made this work possible.

1

WELCOME TO ROUNDUP, MONTANA

Rodney O. Skurdal
Johnny's Coal Road
Roundup, Montana, U.S. of A.
["Without" the United States]

Dear Pastor,

I would like to welcome you to Roundup. What I need to know before I attend the church . . . is what you will be teaching as to our race (Israel) with that of others.

I have not attended any churches for the past fifteen years, due to the fact that the past Pastors have told us that the 'jews' are God's chosen people. . . . I would be "Honored" to attend a true Church that finally teaches us (Israel-white race/Adam) the truth as to who we really are and our relationship with the other races, pursuant to the Word of God, the Holy Scriptures.

Respectfully presented,
Rodney O. Skurdal
from the Tribe of Dan[1]

This letter came to me soon after I arrived in Roundup, Montana, to serve as pastor to my first congregation. The writer of the letter, identifying himself as a member of the Tribe of Dan, was expressing the views of the racial extremist movement known as Christian Identity, more commonly referred to simply as Identity. Basic to the movement is the conviction that the white race is the "seed of Adam" and the biblical Israel that God has chosen.

Racist Christian Identity materials have spawned the growth of numerous militias and support groups. Though also rooted in white supremacist views, their agendas often display a political, antigovernment focus. The number of such groups increased from 224 located in 39 states in 1995 to 809 in 1996 (nearly 300 percent growth in one year), with all states having active organizations. A 1997 report documented the presence and activities of 474 such groups, a 20 percent increase since 1996. Identity racial extremism can now be found coast to coast, from California and its nationally distributed racial publication, the *Jubilee Newspaper*, to Pennsylvania, which is home to a branch of Aryan Nations. This racial theology shows itself not only in such widely known groups as Aryan Nations and some Ku Klux Klan (KKK) groups, but also in the documents filed by groups such as the Montana Freemen. Evidence of these trends is also seen worldwide. Such statistics and trends can sometimes seem far off and impersonal, but in Roundup, Montana, these facts came to me as a personal welcome.[2]

MORE THAN MEETS THE MEDIA'S EYE

On June 13, 1996, the Freemen of Montana were arrested after an eighty-one-day standoff with federal law enforcement officers, the longest in FBI history. In May 1998, fourteen defendants were placed on trial related to a forty-one-count indictment that included conspiracy to commit bank, wire, and mail fraud; filing false claims to the IRS; interstate transportation of stolen property; threatening to kidnap and kill a judge; robbery; and using firearms during a robbery.[3]

The standoff, near the secluded town of Jordan in northeast Montana, became a huge media phenomenon. But the Freemen spent even more time battling what they perceive as the satanic government from a cabin ten miles south of Roundup, about two hours southwest of the publicized standoff. Not until more than a year after my contact with the Freemen, in September 1995, would they put together a well-armed six-car convoy and head north in order to continue their war on the government.

During the Freemen's stay in Roundup, I began to respond to them. It was only two months after I arrived to serve a congregation there, my first position as a pastor. What the media did not know or were not able to access was the racist Identity worldview that drove the Montana Freemen's antigovernment actions.[4] Contrary to popular opinion, the Montana Freemen never claimed to be a militia and never rationalized their existence and actions with appeals to the constitutional right to bear arms. More accurately, they are an Identity group with political, military, and social agendas that are expressions of their Identity faith.

Nestled in the Bull Mountains, Roundup is a gem on the prairies of central Montana that cradles about two thousand residents. It has the typical main street, bars, churches, and ranches. All of these are surrounded and laced through by the Musselshell River, sandstone rimrock, rolling hills, and Bull Mountain pine trees.

Over all, it is a friendly place—even though I wondered how friendly after receiving my letter of welcome from Rodney Skurdal. He is now known as one of the charismatic leaders of the Montana Freemen.[5] At the time he seemed to hold a distorted view of Christianity and to be estranged from the local congregations. I wrote back, "Thank you for your letter and your interest in our church. Let's get together sometime and have coffee."

Although I recognized the racism in the letter, I did not yet realize that his reference to Jews and the white race was part of the comprehensive Identity worldview. I did not yet know that his reference to "white race/Adam" was grounded in the belief that Adam, from the creation accounts of Genesis, was the father of the white race only. And I completely missed that the author, identifying himself as being from the tribe of Dan, was claiming that the biblical lost tribes traveled north and west and inhabited the predominantly white nations of northern Europe.

Even the letter's return address and the lack of a zip code proved significant. To use a zip code, according to the Freemen and similar groups, is to waive one's rights as a sovereign. In response to receiving mail with a zip code from the Montana Department of Revenue one Freeman protested: I am a Private White Individual/ Man/Adam of the "TRIBE OF DAN," of "the lost sheep of the House of Israel." The Freemen believe that the United States (with capital letters) is an illegally established corporation and that Freemen are white males no longer under the jurisdiction of state or federal authorities.[6]

They assert that all amendments ratified after the Bill of Rights of the Constitution were unconstitutional because of Jew-controlled legislative bodies and a Satanic conspiracy. With the ratification of the Fourteenth Amendment of the Constitution in 1868, which granted full citizenship to freed slaves, they maintain that a second class of citizenship was created. The first type of citizenship, which existed before the Fourteenth Amendment, is identified as state or organic citizenship granted to white males. Fourteenth Amendment citizenship applies to people of color and any whites who have signed a contract with the government in the form of a social security card, driver's license, marriage license, income tax form, and so forth. For the Freemen, nearly all the human beings inhabiting the United States are second-class citizens.[7]

I would find out through conversations, underground literature, and research that the Freemen's racial worldview, claims of sovereignty, and extreme localism had some roots that stretched into the Posse Comitatus (Power of the County) movement, which began in the late 1960s. Relying on distorted readings of the Magna Carta, the Articles of Confederation, and the Bill of Rights, the doctrine of the Posse holds that the county sheriff "is the only legal law enforcement officer in these United States of America." A Sheriff's Posse handbook reveals the vigilante behavior prescribed in reaction to any government official thought to have violated the oath of office: "He shall be removed by the Posse to the most populated intersection of streets in the township and at high noon be hung by the neck, the body remaining until sundown as an example." Identity leaders such as Henry "Mike" Beach in Oregon, William Potter Gale in southern California, James Wickstrom of Wisconsin, and Aryan Nations leader Richard Butler contributed significantly to the shaping of the Posse. And Pastor August B. Kreis carries on what Wickstrom began: "This *is* a battle. . . . Yes, a Racial Holy War! . . . We, Yahweh's children ARE His Battle-axe and Weapons of War!" Similar to elements of the Freemen movement, aspects of the early Posse movement were the formation of townships thought to be sovereign communities and clear identification of enemies of the white race, such as the federal government, the IRS, and Jews. Illegal activities including counterfeiting, filing bogus liens, paramilitary training, issuing threats against public officials, and tax protesting spread with the rhetoric. By the late 1980s, Posse activity was less public. Waiting for its next generation of leaders and the right context in which to gain a following, the movement has been described as a dormant volcano that has once again erupted.[8]

The Montana Freemen decided to set up their own common law court in Jordan. The takeover was driven in part by Ralph Clark and his nephew Randy, who would later lend their 960-acre wheat farm, on which by 1995 they owed $1.8 million in back payments, to the Freemen for the formation of Justus Township. With Richard Clark purporting to act as presiding judge, in the presence of about three dozen others, the Freemen marched into the Garfield County Courthouse to create their own government. Clark announced to those gathered at the meeting: "We've opened our own common law court and we have the law back in the county now." Soon afterward posters appeared offering a bounty of one million dollars for the arrest of the county sheriff, the county attorney, and the judge. And in March 1995 the Freemen published a public notice in the local newspaper claiming they would be taking control of large portions of northeastern Montana including Bureau of Land Management property, state grazing lands, and some privately owned lands. The notice included threats that those who trespassed would be arrested and punished.[9]

The Musselshell County jail was the site of my next encounter with the Freemen. As I stepped up to the mesh-wire cell door, I was greeted by an incarcerated Mr. Skurdal and another Freeman. It quickly became clear that the men viewed me as part of the deceived, government-controlled church. The fact that our church had signed a non-profit, tax exemption contract with the satanic government disqualified us from legitimacy and put us under the control of the federal government: "The purported state created churches, those who have a tax exempt 501(c) form, will not teach 'Israel' [read: white race] the truth, for they are there to mislead the masses into the new world order."[10]

During our discussion, the two men frequently claimed secret knowledge. For example, that day they told me that after becoming president during the Great Depression, Franklin Roosevelt, a pawn of the Jew-controlled conspiracy, seized powers under the Trading with the Enemy Act (1917) and the Emergency Banking Act (1933), passed to regulate wartime financial transactions. Since that time, they asserted, the Constitution has been suspended, a state of emergency has remained in force, and U.S. citizens are living under martial law and an unconstitutional dictatorship run from Washington, D.C.

Despite the outlandish nature of such claims, the jailed men who espoused them looked like ordinary businessmen, farmers, or ranchers. Identity racial extremists believe in a world that makes perfect sense to them.[11]

What if you believed that the government was a seemingly all-powerful evil entity, foreign troops were gathering at the borders set to invade, the United Nations (UN) could control the weather, and people of color and Jews were out to destroy your race? How do you compromise with people who believe that you want to seize their land, take their guns, and throw them into concentration camps? What if you believed that what has driven history is a gigantic conspiracy set in motion by demonic forces, and that what is at stake is not this or that political view but a battle between good and evil? In 1997 such a worldview drove members of a racial militia to obtain machine guns and plot attacks on U.S. military bases suspected of harboring and training UN troops. If one looks through the lens of Identity, an officer performing a seemingly routine traffic stop ceases to be a human being and becomes a symbol of a satanic government, and the stop can turn into a battle to the death against pawns of the government.[12]

During my jail visit that day, the Freemen and I frequently cited the Bible. But in the days and weeks to come I became convinced that hurling scripture quotes back and forth like grenades would not be helpful in significantly addressing Identity racial extremism. The problem we faced in communicating with one another was deeper and more profound. The center of their faith and life was fundamentally opposed to the center of faith and life for the Christian church. Theirs was a fundamentally different confession of faith.

VISITS WITH AN IDENTITY FAMILY

My next encounter with Identity extremism came with a man I met during a jail visit. Bill (not his real name) was likable and quick to smile. As we visited, we discussed matters important to a man who was incarcerated and had a family waiting for him on the outside. Before Bill was released, he asked me to visit his wife, Betty, and their children. Betty welcomed me into their home. She showed deep concern for her husband, the task of home-schooling the kids, and trying to make ends meet. She asked for prayer and hoped that Bill would soon be released so that they could get on with their lives. As I leaned up against their kitchen counter before leaving, my hand landed on a booklet, which, judging by the cover, was an Aryan publication, a racial booklet. Betty quickly dismissed the work as something given to her husband by a friend.

Later I discovered the family had a history of involvement in racial extremist activities in northwest Montana. I visited Bill and Betty quite regularly, and many of our conversations focused on the profound differences between Identity's racial theology and the Christian faith. Bill was intrigued by my focus on God's grace: "It's God's grace that makes Christians, not race. The love of Christ makes Christians." Bill gave me racial material to study and prepare for our next discussion, and more than once he wanted me to meet some people with whom he was studying.[13]

After Bill invited me to meet the study leaders, Betty must have thought I was uncomfortable with the proposal and assured me that I would fit right in because I was a tall, blond, blue-eyed Aryan. During one of our discussions, Bill's voice grew hushed as he revealed he was part American Indian, as if he was confessing a sin. He was living with doubt concerning his genetic link to the Chosen race.

Racial purity and the preservation of the white race are essential to the Identity movement. One example illustrates the concern for racial purity. Dan Gayman of the Church of Israel, an Identity community in Missouri, answers readers' questions in their publication, *The Watchman:*

> Question: Pastor Gayman, is there major variation in the hair, eye, and skin color of Israelites [read: whites]? If I have incomplete or scanty genealogical records, how can I be sure that I am a pure Israelite?
>
> Answer: Historically, if you could pass the blue blood test, you were considered white. That is, the blood veins had to be apparent to the eye, a test generally observed by rolling up the sleeve of the shirt and noting the blood veins showing through the skin. . . . It is unfortunate that no genealogical records are available for most Israelites in this generation. Complete racial history is sometimes scanty, making many live by faith that they are racially pure. If it is obvious by skin color that someone is not Caucasian, appropriate steps can be taken by Church leadership to preserve the racial integrity of the congregation.[14]

One spring morning Bill invited me to ride with him to the family ranch he was refurbishing. We had a beautiful morning drive through the Bull Mountains, and then he set out to feed his horses while we talked. Still at times I was taken aback by Bill's virulent Identity rhetoric. In passing, I referred to Bill's children as kids. "They are not kids," he shot back, obviously offended. He assured me that his children were no "beasts of the field," apparently a reference to the Identity belief that people of color were inferior beasts (Gen. 1:30 KJV).[15]

Overall, however, his Identity rhetoric was becoming less frequent, and on the way back to Roundup, Bill expressed concern about getting involved with the Freemen. Not long after our day together, six Freemen and the leader of the Militia of Montana, the Roundup Seven, were arrested in Roundup, accused of planning to kidnap the Musselshell County judge and hang him in retaliation for the arrest and conviction of another Freeman. The arrests, just a month and a half before the Oklahoma City bombing, hit the communication networks of militia and Patriot groups already frantic with rumors of mass arrests set for March 25. Those seeing a conspiracy asserted that the arrests were "the start of a well-orchestrated crackdown on militias and other patriotic groups all across America." The Musselshell County sheriff and county attorney's offices were inundated with threatening phone calls.[16]

The next time I saw Bill he had landed in the county jail again. His would be a short stay, and ours would be a short conversation. Bill told me that he and his wife had been attending a Christian church in Billings. His eyes grew larger as he said, "Pastor, when we were leaving church last week, I walked up to a black woman and gave her a big hug, my sister in Christ." To make such a confession of faith, Bill had to be looking at the world very differently from before, through the lens of a different faith.

A RUDE WAKE-UP CALL

People living out of the Identity racial worldview have given a rude wake-up call for us to think and talk seriously about religion as a force that affects public and personal life. As racial extremists thrust their views into the public arena, the religious convictions that undergird their racial world affect our lives. Clearly, our so-called private beliefs shape our lives together; they actually matter.

The danger in being so reminded is that we might react in a knee-jerk manner, asserting that religious convictions should not matter, especially in the public realm. But this reaction would only extend a pervading ethos in our country that acting on religious beliefs to affect public life is somehow oppressive or even wicked. Like latter-day Freudians, it seems many regard deep religious conviction as a symptom of neurosis.

This book goes the other way. The number and size of racial extremist groups have grown. Only by embracing religious convictions and the way in which they shape persons and groups can we expose Identity's racist theology and examine its contents in order to get more accurate information about the motives and goals of such groups and respond in engaging, effective ways.

No fringe racial extremist group should be persecuted for religious beliefs. The Freemen and other groups are free to believe in a racial god whose white race is the true Israel. But because they speak does not mean that we must heed their call or permit their vision to prevail. And I hope, with a mighty hope, that theirs is not the only voice out there. Toward that end, this book lifts up the witness of the Christian church as a reference point for discussion.

IDENTITY EXTREMISM AND THE TIMES

On the one hand, the blight of Identity extremism exposed in this book should not cause one to despair that we now live in the worst of times. On the other hand, the radically dehumanizing racial extremism that most only hear about, read about, or see in the movies has intensified. Neither the alarmists nor the social optimists should cheer just yet. Human history, with all of its developments and discoveries, has not changed the basic narcissism of individuals, races, or nations that "practically everyone is expendable except ourselves." Some have claimed that the twentieth century is "the most violent century in history."[17] Racial extremism has mutated but is still a part of our shared human condition.

What is prompting this mutation and resurgence? Explanations include the disparity between social classes, disappointment in a failed American Dream, and the lost paradise promised by commercial industrialism. Those who speak of a single cause should be avoided, and those looking for a single cause will be disappointed. The mutation and resurgence of racial extremism are complex, as the following explanations reveal.

Some observers point to the economic conditions surrounding the Posse Comitatus movement. The rise of this group seems to coincide with the U.S. farm crisis that began in the 1970s, when low crop prices, high interest rates, foreclosures, accelerated repayment schedules, and bankruptcies bred desperation, mistrust, and hatred. By 1983 North Dakota alone was losing three farmers a day: "The sharp report of the auctioneer's gavel echoed across the prairie . . . the death knell to a way of life." Though inadequate as either an explanation or an excuse, such an economic-social cluster seems to be a part of extremism. And myriad factors continue to endanger traditional industries such as mining, ranching, and logging.[18]

Others point to increased federal authority over states' rights to explain the current rise and spread of racial extremism. The government's watch over our lives has resulted in the passage of 1,397 federal laws and resolutions and the writing of 62,928 pages of regulations in one year. Some include in this tally government corruption and misdeeds. Most often mentioned are complicity in the death of the wife of Randy Weaver during the 1992 standoff at Ruby Ridge, Idaho, and the deaths of nearly one hundred men, women, and children during the Branch Davidian standoff in Waco, Texas, in 1993.[19]

Still others, thinking in a more apocalyptic manner, suggest that, with the end of the cold war and the demise of the Soviet Union having left us without an external enemy, perhaps we need a new target for our fears and are looking for the enemy in our midst. Or perhaps people, no longer able to cope with unwanted and feared social changes (including the dizzying rate of the increase in technology), need to demonize other human beings to explain their plight. Or perhaps Caucasians, having held a position of privilege for several centuries, are constructing for themselves, as the Nazis did before them, "a mythical hero system . . . in order to earn a feeling of primary value, of cosmic specialness, of ultimate usefulness to creation, of unshakable meaning." Martin Luther King Jr. in 1963 pointed out that, "lamentably, it is a historical fact that privileged groups seldom give up their privileges voluntarily" and that "groups tend to be more immoral than individuals." Or perhaps at least a few in such movements are motivated to make money. Catalogs are distributed including video and audio tapes, books, military supplies, tax protesting kits, T-shirts, caps, and other essentials needed to fight the satanic government.[20]

All these theories have some plausibility. Underlying them, and perhaps what can hold them together, are insights about the human condition. To effectively suppress the terrors of our limitations and inevitable deaths, we construct comprehensive worldviews to deny these and attempt "to forget the pathetic creature that man is" this side of Eden.[21]

My basic perspective is theological—and with good reason. Identity extremism in its most virulent form claims that Jews are the offspring of Satan and Eve, and that people of color are animal-like beasts of the field. In contrast, the white race is the true Israel of the Bible, and Jesus came to save only his kinsmen, the white race. These are all theological claims. The Christian church must respond early and effectively to racial extremism, the misuse of the Bible to shape this racial worldview, and misrepresentation of the gospel of Jesus Christ. Such a response will be grounded neither in psychological evaluations of those whose charisma or law breaking attracts the media's spotlight nor in social or historical investigation (although a wise theologian will use these tools). This book then exposes Identity racial extremism and its allied forces as the encounter of two centers: the center of faith and life for Identity racial extremism and the center of faith and life for the Christian church.

2

GOD AND THE CREATION OF RACISM

Remember that the Bible was written for only one race of people.

—Freeman Edict

Identity racism is shaped by a particular reading of the creation accounts in the first chapters of the first book of the Bible, Genesis. Put together, these beliefs form a clear theology that is contrary to Judaism and Christianity. Here are some of Identity's core commitments:

1. The different races have their origins in separate creations by God (polygenesis).
2. People of color (nonwhites) were created before Adam and Eve, are less endowed spiritually, and do not share in redemption.
3. Adam and Eve were the first white people created by God, were endowed with exceptional spiritual capacities, and were specially chosen by God; white descendants of Adam and Eve share these same capacities and election.
4. Present-day Jews are descendants of Satan and Eve and are fundamentally opposed to God and God's purposes.
5. Race mixing was the original sin in the Garden of Eden and the source of the white race's woes outside the garden, which led to the Flood—and the current need for racial separation.

THE BEASTS OF THE FIELD

Identity racists are convinced that the Bible is God's revelation concerning the races and that "the Bible was written for only one race of people."[1] To be sure, a wide spectrum of movements are counted in Identity—from those spearheaded by the former Grand Wizard of the Ku Klux Klan and politician David Duke to the founder and leader of Aryan Nations, Richard Girnt Butler. But they share this basic conviction and conclusion.

The groups that are in the Identity category, then, cannot be characterized as consisting of people who, in the words of one prominent Identity pastor, "fall into the religious right."[2] Their virulent racism clearly precludes this. Neither are they merely tax protesters or antigovernment activists, although many do protest taxes and often oppose the federal government. Identity churches and communities such as the Montana Freemen, Laporte Church of Christ in Colorado,[3] and American Christian Ministries[4] in Medford, Oregon, adhere to and live out of dehumanizing forms of racial theology. It can be shown that every other commitment they espouse—however unconnected from other parts of their agenda it may seem at first—flows from the belief that the Bible was written for the white race only.

Taking the narrative from Genesis in order, Identity extremism alleges that the first creation narrative (Gen. 1–2:4) is an account of God's creating inferior, *pre-Adamic* (that is, born before Adam) people of color. Such persons of color are less endowed spiritually and intellectually, they maintain, than the Adamic white race, which was placed later on earth.[5]

But was not humankind created in the "image of God" (Gen. 1:27)? According to the Montana Freemen, this refers to the dark people of color: "The first men, both male and female, were created in God's shadow or image, dark color." Also, according to Identity doctrine, pre-Adamic people are without souls: "These men [plural] were created at the same time, male and female. . . . These men, males and females, did not receive the breath of life, or that special spirit, electrical energy, or a soul (Gen. 1:27)."[6] And because translations of this first creation account (Gen. 1–2:4) lack the distinctive words for the male and female (Adam and Eve) found in Genesis 2, these pre-Adamic people are claimed to somehow be more generic, "stamped out," and inferior to the Adamic white race. Also lifted from these early verses of Genesis is that people of color are referred to as "beasts of the field" (Gen. 3:1 KJV). The non-Aryans, it is alleged, were created along with and are on the same level as animals such as cattle and birds;[7] these "beasts" were "soulless people of color."[8]

The search for references to "beasts of the field" elsewhere in the Bible, for them, seems to substantiate this interpretation. For example, in the laws of the book of Leviticus, bestiality, or sexual relations with an animal, is prohibited. Identity extremists interpret this as God's command forbidding Aryans to race mix. In fact, race mixing was punishable by death: "If a man lie with a beast [read: person of color], he shall surely be put to death: and ye shall slay the beast. And if a woman approach unto any beast, and lie down thereto, thou shalt kill the woman, and the beast" (Lev. 20:15–16 KJV).[9] To lend a scientific aura to the biblical claims, racial extremists often cite evidence they claim is irrefutable.[10] That this racial theology is ever disputed is looked upon as a ploy to raise up the "false doctrine" of the equality of races.[11]

THE ADAMIC WHITE RACE

Turning to Genesis 2, Identity adherents assert that the Adamic white race was specially created, favored by God from the beginning. This creation account (Gen. 2:4–25), which follows the well-known seven-day creation story, is read as a fluid continuation of those seven days. It follows then that since "on the seventh day God finished the work that God had done, and God rested" (Gen. 2:2), Adam, the first white man, was "formed from the ground on the eighth day"[12] of creation and placed by God in the cradle prepared for the white race. Adam was "the father of only one race on this earth, that is the Caucasian race": "We believe God chose unto himself a special race of people that are above all people upon the face of the earth. . . . We believe the White, Anglo-Saxon, Germanic and kindred people to be God's true, literal Children of Israel."[13] This main tenet of Identity, the "Israel Truth" that the white race was chosen from creation and constitutes biblical Israel, pervades most Identity works:

- The Israel Truth is the key that opens up the Bible from the first promise made at the Fall, until Jesus delivers up the finished Kingdom to the Father.[14]
- The key to understanding the Bible is the truth that we [read: the white race] are Israelites.[15]
- God breathed life into Adam (Gen. 2:7) "giving him a higher

form of consciousness and distinguishing him from all the other races of the earth."[16]

In this second creation account (Gen. 2:4–25), the personal nouns Adam and Eve are used for the first time. The meaning of the Hebrew word for Adam is thought to support the divine elevation of the white race because, Identity adherents argue, "Adam . . . means: ruddy, to show blood in the face, flush or turn rosy, to be able to blush, to be fair."[17] In any case, creation expands around Adam until finally woman, Eve, is created and brought to Adam and the two become one (Gen. 2:18–25).

THE TWO-SEED THEORY AND SATAN'S KIDS

The harmony of Adam and Eve's partnership and marriage is short-lived, however, because according to Identity doctrine, a satanic sexual seducer lurked in Eden (Gen. 3:1–7). This portion of Genesis is traditionally known as the Fall. But for Identity disciples, the two-seed theory of the origins of humankind emerges. "The serpent" appears on the scene (Gen. 3:1) and converses with Eve concerning the trees God planted in the center of the garden, and questions the prohibition by God concerning the fruit of the "tree of knowledge of good and evil." Eventually, both Adam and Eve disobey God, partake of the fruit, and are judged by God for their rebellion.

The importance of Genesis 3—and more particularly Genesis 3:15—for Identity theology cannot be overstated. Addressed to the serpent and found in the judgment section of the narrative (3:14–19), Genesis 3:15 reads: "I will put enmity between you and the woman, and between your offspring and hers." Identity adherents assert that what is revealed in this verse is a genetic hatred between the Adamic white race and Satan's offspring, the Jews. The claim is that in the garden there was a "counterfeit incarnation" by Satan, whose plan was to perpetuate his own seed-line and whose descendants, contrary to God's plans, would pass themselves off as the true Israel of the Bible. The Identity book *The Two Seeds of Genesis 3:15* calls this verse "the key that unlocks the Bible."[18]

> If you were to select one verse in the Bible that gives its most complete summary, Genesis 3:15 would be that verse. If you capture a vision of this verse and move forth conceptually . . . you will put all of the pieces of the puzzle together.[19]

Identity asserts that there are two lines of descendants originating from Eve. Adam and Eve had sexual relations, they assert, and their offspring was Abel, who was killed by Cain and replaced by Seth. From Adam and in turn Seth's descendants came the white race, the true Israel, the chosen people of God: "The unconditional election of a people named Israel . . . from the race of Adam is a cornerstone of Bible teaching."[20] Because pure-blood descendants are from the seed-line of Adam, the first white man, these descendants are inherently good. But another seed-line originates in the garden, they say. Eve also had sexual relations with the serpent or a humanoid satanic being. The offspring of Eve and Satan was Cain, the first Jew, a literal child of Satan on earth. Cain and his offspring are genetically evil: "We believe in an existing being known as the Devil or Satan and called the Serpent . . . who has a literal seed or posterity in the earth . . . commonly called Jews today."[21]

According to this theory, the world contains descendants of Adam and descendants of Satan, a kind of incarnational dualism, good and evil right down on earth, which is the source of a life-and-death struggle between Satan's descendants and the children of God.[22] (See diagram 1.) Racism and anti-Semitism have existed for centuries in one form and degree of severity or another. But one cannot dehumanize or demonize any human being more than this:

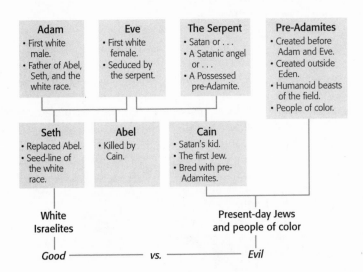

Diagram 1: Identity Seed-Lines and Incarnational Dualism.

"Cain, made in the image and likeness of Satan, took on the nature of Satan's evil and sinful ways. Cain was the personification of sin."[23] The claim is that present-day Jews are literally demonic, genetically and spiritually, and because of their heredity, are the natural enemies of the white race.[24] Identity adherents are essentially saying that there are those who are outside the realm and power of God's love and mercy given in Jesus Christ. Heaven has been assaulted by these new racial extremists, and hell opened ready to receive its nonwhites; baptism cannot save the Jews, they believe, because they are Satan's kids.

The sexual seduction that would lead to the satanic seed-line begins with Genesis 3:1: "Now the serpent was more subtle than any beast of the field which the Lord God had made" (KJV). The word for "serpent"—using a very creative combination of etymology, Arabic, and word association—is concluded to be Satan, a lower helper of Satan such as a "handsome angel,"[25] or a two-legged "beast of the field" possessed by Satan to do Satan's bidding.[26] The pamphlet *In the Image of God* concludes that the serpent was an exceptional "beast of the field" used by Satan for evil purposes: "Satan made use of this creature as the most proper instrument for the accomplishment of his murderous purposes against the life and soul of man. Under this creature he lay hid, and by this creature he seduced our first parents. We have here a genuine clue in full support of the deduction that [the serpent], a highly intelligent beast of the field, was a purebred Negro."[27]

One Identity interpreter confidently concludes, "Any other interpretation for the serpent denies the reality of the Bible."[28] And any other conclusion has elsewhere been described as "undoubtedly the greatest hoax in history."[29] Having established the sinister or satanic origin of the serpent and its humanoid form, Identity regards as another key to interpretation the discussion of the trees in the center of the garden and the forbidden fruit from the tree of the knowledge of good and evil.

In Identity theology, the serpent as tempter becomes the serpent as sexual seducer, developed with a metaphorical interpretation of the trees and fruit in the garden, the two trees planted representing the bodily presence of God and Satan (Gen. 2:9): "The 'tree' in the garden was in fact the 'serpent,' a.k.a. Satan, the Dragon, the Devil, the Arch-Angel, Lucifer."[30] And Eve, like all women, it is asserted, in being susceptible to giving in to her lower faculties, chose the "tree" that was pleasant to the eyes, took, and ate. In the words of an Identity minister in a taped lecture: "It wasn't an apple in the hand of Eve as the so-called Christian churches claim, but it was a pear [read: pair] on the ground."[31] The Montana Freemen put it this way: "Now you can visualize a beautiful garden with two men in it, one being Yhvh [God] (the tree of life) who was not strikingly handsome, the other man however, Satan (the tree of Knowledge, of both good and evil) was good looking and desirable to Eve, also good for food and eating or partaking of him." The Genesis narrative goes on to tell us that after Adam and Eve disobeyed God and partook of the forbidden fruit, their "eyes were opened"; they realized that they were naked and "sewed fig leaves together and made loincloths for themselves" (Gen. 3:7). Reasoning from the two-seed theory, Identity states, "If, as the so-called churches would have you believe, their sin was eating the forbidden fruit, why did they not put the fig leaf over their mouth?"[32]

Next, Adam and Eve are questioned by God (Gen. 3:11), and both point beyond themselves to assign the responsibility for their disobedience. Adam blames God and Eve, and in turn Eve blames the serpent, who "tricked" her (Gen. 3:13) or, Identity claims, sexually seduced her. For Identity, the sin in the garden that resulted in the fall of humankind and a broken relationship with God was not humankind's disobeying the word of God and wanting to be more like the Creator than like the creatures they were created to be. The sin in the garden was not Adam and Eve's inability to live out of trust. For Identity adherents, looking through the lens of the two-seed theory of the origins of humankind, the sin in the garden, the original sin, was race mixing—in Hitler's words, "blood sin and desecration of the race."[33]

And the responsibility for this sin rests with Eve: "In original sin, Satan was able to physically seduce the woman Eve. . . . Cain was the bastard, spurious seed that resulted from their cohabitation."[34] Because Eve committed the great sin of race mixing, Eve, Adam, and the whole human race must face a battle with the seed of the serpent for the life of God's chosen white race. Adam's sin is explained in sexual terms as well, but it seems an afterthought to include him in the responsibility for the broken relationship with God. Identity theology claims that Adam's sin was to have sexual relations with Eve after she had defiled herself with Satan.

> What, then, was Adam's sin in having conjugal relations with his wife? First, Adam knew that the woman had been seduced by Satan. Second, Adam knew that the woman was fallen from glory and immortality and now existed in a

body of sin. Third, Adam knew that to join with his wife in physical intimacy in her state of sin would incur the wrath of God.[35]

A simple reading of Genesis 4:1 would seem to reveal that Cain could be none other than Adam and Eve's offspring. Genesis 4:1 reads, "Now the man knew his wife Eve, and she conceived and bore Cain, saying, 'I have produced a man with the help of God.'" Even an Identity adherent admits that "at first glance, one would assume that Cain was the offspring of this man and wife."[36] First, that the Bible states only once that Adam *knew* (in this case the verb refers to sexual relations) his wife (Gen. 4:1) is taken as proof that Adam was the father of only one child, Abel, and not Cain. One explanation offered by Identity is that Eve was deceived by Satan into thinking that she had begotten a son with a messenger from God, an angel of light (see 2 Cor. 11:14), who was in fact Satan in disguise. Cain and Abel are related, Identity adherents would say, but only through their mother. They are the offspring of different fathers.[37]

All of the punishments given by God because of Eve's disobedience are integrated into Identity interpretation. For example, the serpent was cursed to crawl upon its belly and to eat the dust all the days of its life (Gen. 3:14). "If the serpent was a snake," one Identity interpretation asks, "why would God say that he was to crawl on his belly, he must not have crawled before the event."[38] And the perpetual enmity between the offspring of the serpent and the offspring of Eve (Gen. 3:15) represents the division among races, and for some Identity adherents, divine sanction to do battle.

THE FIRST JEW: A MURDERER AND A LIAR

Genesis 4 contains the story of the brothers (half brothers, Identity would assert) Cain and Abel (Gen. 4:1–26) and the further unfolding of the histories of the seed-line of Adam and the seed-line of Satan. In the course of time Cain and Abel bring offerings before God, Cain from the fruit of the ground, and Abel from the firstlings of his flock. The Bible tells us that "God had regard for Abel and his offering, but for Cain and his offering God had no regard" (Gen. 4:4–5).

Through the lens of the two-seed theory, it stands to reason that God would reject Cain's offering; Cain was the offspring of Satan and at enmity with God and God's purposes. Satan, through Cain and his descendants, was out to thwart the purposes of God for the

Adamic white race and the world. It would be preposterous to think that God would even consider Cain's offering: "God accepted the offering from Abel, but rejected the offering of Cain because he was unworthy, that is, he was of the serpent."[39]

After Cain's offering is rejected, he entices Abel to "go out to the field" with him, and there he kills him (Gen. 4:8). As Satan's off-spring, Cain has the natural inclination to be a murderer. This act of Cain is taken to be the beginning of the "enmity" between the races spoken of in Genesis 3:15, "the first overt expression of the enmity or hatred" between the seed of the serpent and the seed of Adam.[40] After killing Abel, Cain acts true to his nature as Satan's kid and lies about his heinous act. When God asks where Abel is, Cain answers, "I do not know; am I my brother's keeper?" (Gen. 4:9). Murder and lies are also parts of the racial urge of the present-day Jew, Identity adherents contend.[41]

Through Identity's interpretation of Genesis 4 and the role of Cain, certain questions are brought to the text and answered. One such question is where Cain might have obtained a wife if Adam and Eve were the first human beings created by God. "If there were no other peoples on the earth who was Cain afraid of? . . . Cain was cast out, who did he marry if there were no other people?"[42] The Identity answer is that Adam and Eve were not the first people created; there were pre-Adamic people of color whose existence outside the Aryan cradle answers the questions regarding Cain's wife and associations. Cain "went away from the presence of God, and settled in the land of Nod, east of Eden" (Gen. 4:16), and in Nod, Identity adherents claim, he intermarried with the pre-Adamic people of color.[43] And because of his superior, albeit satanic origins, Cain became a great leader among the pre-Adamites. He was the source of idol and devil worship, decadent secular civiliza-tion, and through his seed-line, all that is opposed to God. Cain comes to loom over Identity theology and history in ways that far outweigh his actual role in the Genesis narratives and the Bible as a whole.[44] Selections from Identity material corroborate these Cainite interpretations:

> We believe that the Adam-man of Genesis was the placing of the White race upon this earth. Not all races descend from Adam. Adam is the father of the White race only. . . . We believe that there are literal children of Satan in the world today. These children are the descendants of Cain, who was a result of Eve's original sin, her physical seduction

by Satan. We know that because of this sin there is a battle and a natural enmity between the children of Satan and the children of The Most High God.[45]

We believe the White, Anglo-Saxon, Germanic and kindred people to be God's true, literal Children of Israel. Only this race fulfills every detail of Biblical Prophecy and World History concerning Israel. . . . We believe in an existing being known as the Devil or Satan and called the Serpent, who has literal "seed" or posterity in the earth commonly called Jews today.[46]

THE FLOOD: PUNISHMENT FOR RACE MIXING

Interpretation of the Bible in racial terms continues with the narrative of Noah and the Flood (Gen. 6:1–8:22). Identity adherents claim that the Flood was geographically localized, a punishment by God inflicted on the Adamic race, not for general wickedness but for the specific sin of race mixing.[47] Using unsubstantiated historical information including a long-standing myth concerning the origins of the Aryan race, Identity adherents believe that the Adamic race was created in a mountain-ringed basin in present-day central China.[48] While the pre-Adamic "beasts of the field" roamed the lowlands outside the mountain-ringed basin, God's chosen white race was placed in a cradle to preserve racial integrity and spiritual stature.

Seclusion was not total, however, and Identity adherents use brief biblical references to legendary supernatural "sons of God" and "daughters of humans" during a pre-Flood period to assert that Adamic white males were guilty of venturing out of the God-given cradle and race mixing with pre-Adamic women (Gen. 6:2, 4).[49] At first only a few Adamites ventured out, they claim, but eventually many more wives were chosen from pre-Adamic races. Because of the sin of race mixing and the threat posed to the spiritual stature of the Adamic race, God punished the Adamic race by flooding the mountain-ringed basin.[50] But because of God's covenant with Adam, and because Noah was "a thoroughbred, not a mongrel," God permitted a remnant, Noah and his family, to survive. Upon receiving instruction from God and being "a survivalist," Noah built the ark and preserved the Adamic race.[51]

There are some variations to these formulations, but what is held in common is a consistently racial interpretation of the Flood.

Some claim that God punished the pre-Adamites because of the increasing and alluring danger of race mixing. Others claim that the "sons of God" were sinister beings that possessed Adamic men and coerced them into taking wives from among the pre-Adamites. And still others claim that the Flood was universal, that quite literally "waters swelled so mightily on the earth that all the high mountains under the whole heaven were covered" (Gen. 7:19). Yet in this scenario, in keeping with the promise of enmity given in Genesis 3:15, Cain's seed must have survived the Flood by entering the ark among the pairs of "all flesh" (Gen. 6:19–20). When Noah boarded the ark, the "seed of the serpent" entered as "unclean flesh": "The Seed . . . survived the flood. . . . [They] are not, of course, Adamic Seed and therefore were not counted among Noah and his family or as 'people.'"[52]

This racial interpretation of Genesis is the lens through which Identity reads the rest of the Bible and sees all of faith and life. Religious racists are often accused of pulling one or two verses out of the Bible and basing their whole worldview on them, but this is not really the case with Identity theology. Although these racial extremists do read certain verses out of context, they interpret and operate from a center. They have a hermeneutic, a lens through which to read the Scriptures. And based on this hermeneutic, their interpretation has some coherence as will be evidenced in following chapters. Who is left that thinks the end of the aberration of racism that blossomed in the 1930s and 1940s has finally been reached? The ideology, indeed the theology, of modern racism has developed and gone further in its incorporation of the pieces and people of the Bible and of our world.

3

GREAT NATIONS
FOR WHITES ONLY

Let's tell our children the truth about Israel—that we Anglo-Saxon, Celtic, Germanic, and kindred peoples are the true descendants of the twelve sons of Israel, and that our great nation and the great Christian nations of Europe are the nations promised to the seed of Abraham, Isaac, and Jacob.

—Sheldon Emry[1]

God's call to Abram (whose name God later changed to Abraham) is a watershed event in the Hebrew Scriptures. The story of creation describes God's calling into being the whole of the cosmos and places God's election of Abraham in the humbling context of God's providential care of all that exists (Gen. 12:1–25:18). With God's gracious call of Abraham we have the very genesis of the faith of Israel. God chose Abraham to raise up a people for God and to further God's plans for a covenant with all nations (Gen. 12:1–3). But for Identity adherents, the covenant that God made with Abraham was for the white race only.

THE CALL OF ABRAHAM AND THE LOST TRIBES

Following Abraham's encounter with God are a number of *theophanies*—instances when God appears to God's people to significantly direct, instruct, and bless them. God reveals God's self to Isaac, Abraham's son, and then to Jacob, Isaac's son. God repeats the promises and covenants made with Abraham, and promises a future with God. Because God remains faithful, all of the promises made

22

to Abraham had to do with the future of Jacob's children. The rest of the Hebrew Scriptures deals almost exclusively with these heirs of the promises, Jacob's children, otherwise known in the Bible as the children of Israel. One reading of the Hebrew Scriptures accepted by Christians and Jews is that Israel was chosen to be "a light to the nations" (Isa. 42:6)—"nations" meaning places containing other races—so that God's name will "resound through all the earth" (Exod. 9:16).

Seen through the lens of Identity, in contrast, the promises given to Abraham and his descendants were meant for the white race only. In the booklet *Heirs of the Promise*,[2] this racial interpretation is explained beginning with Adam and through Abraham to the time that the northern kingdom of Israel was taken into captivity by Assyria (2 Kings 18:9–12). With a combination of creative archeology, revisionist history, and sweeping claims to biblical proof, it is concluded: "The so-called 'lost tribes of Israel' really were never lost. . . . They migrated onto the continent of Europe and were the ancestors of the white, European race."[3] Maps circulate in Identity circles that trace the migration of the lost tribes north and west to northern Europe and eventually across the Atlantic Ocean to the United States.[4]

In this worldview every marvel and mystery is attributed to the wisdom and skill of the white race: Stonehenge in England, the great pyramids of Egypt, the Taj Mahal in India. Louisiana politician and former Ku Klux Klan leader David Duke's romantic reflections on the accomplishments of Aryans, although pessimistic about the future, are typical: "A feeling came over me as I viewed the Taj Mahal in the sunlight. The rounded dome with its white, bone-like features resembled a huge skull, symbolizing the spiritual cranium of the Aryan people, one that once housed and held talented and powerful minds; but which now only served as a magnificent gravestone of a high culture and genetic treasure that is no more."[5]

Identity materials are laced with such claims as "there would be no civilization at all"[6] if it were not for the white race. This high calling given by God is "white man's burden." "God bestowed upon that one race almost every invention and discovery that has improved man's condition and lot upon the earth. Certainly, God made these offspring of Abraham a blessing to all the families of the earth."[7] Identity theologians claim that tracing the seed of Adam to the United States, among other destinations, is "akin to tracking a rich vein of gold through a mountain."[8] They leave behind "a perfect set of fingerprints" to identify them as biblical Israel.[9]

Identifying the fingerprints of the lost tribes is a common and vital endeavor for Identity adherents.[10] One fingerprint "proving" the white race is Israel is that it fulfills the promise that Abraham's descendants would be "as numerous as the stars of heaven and as the sand that is on the seashore" (Gen. 22:17). Identity claims that the Anglo-Saxon community of kindred nations "is the only people on the face of the earth that meets these criteria."[11] Another Identity fingerprint is the presence of a monarchy that can be traced from the time of King David, which they believe is now being occupied by Queen Elizabeth and the royal family of Great Britain. The queen of England and her children, they claim, enjoy a genetic link that can be traced to the biblical kings of Israel[12] and live in the place from which Christianity began: "Christianity has historically been associated with a particular group of people; . . . Caucasian Israelites."[13] By claiming that the promises in the Hebrew Scriptures from creation through Abraham, David, and all of history are promises fulfilled through and for the white race, Identity adherents add to the language and symbols of racism the implication that they have the blessing and sanction of all the prominent figures of the Hebrew Scriptures and, looking forward to the Christian Scriptures, the blessing and sanction of Jesus.

JEWS AND GENTILES IN THE CHRISTIAN SCRIPTURES

Identity theology uses the words "Jew" and "Gentile" in distinctive ways. The word "Jew" is used in ways that create vagueness and allow fluidity in application.[14] First, "Jew" can be the label for someone who is from the country of Judea.[15] Identity adherents claim that Jesus was given the title of "King of the Jews" by the Roman authorities and others (Mark 15:18–26), and Jesus said, "Salvation is from the Jews" (John 4:22), merely because of Jesus' birth in Bethlehem of Judea (Matt. 2:5; Luke 2:11), a strictly geographical reference.[16] After all, they say, Jesus could not have possibly "come out of a race which hates Christianity."[17] Jesus could just as well have been called Jesus of Nazareth, as he is nineteen times in the Christian Scriptures.[18] And Jesus, who spent most of his life in the area of Galilee, could have most accurately been called Jesus the Galilean. If we look on the term as strictly geographical, it follows that Jesus' followers were not Jews but were Galileans: "Galileans, not Jews, became Christians!"[19]

Second, for Identity adherents, the term "Jew" can designate a distinct race of people as long as it is not applied to Jesus or his disciples. In contrast to Jesus' disciples, who are mistakenly called

Jews, those among Jesus' opponents who were Jews are designated as such because they are biological descendants of the devil. Identity claims that during Jesus' lifetime and through the first century when the Christian Scriptures were taking shape, "the Serpent Seed dominated both the Pharisees and the Sadducees."[20] And as we leave the seed of the serpent found in the Christian Scriptures and move through history, the offspring of Satan seem to be even more recognizable by the term "Jew": "A vast majority of those calling themselves Jews today . . . are descended from the Canaanites, Edomites, Mongolians, Khazars, and Huns. . . . While these people call themselves Jews, the Bible makes clear that they are of the synagogue of Satan."[21]

Third, Identity doctrine uses the term "Jew" to refer to a specific ungodly religion. Adherents claim that during the exile of the southern kingdom of Judah by Babylon, there arose a distinct satanic religion corrupted by pagan Babylonian beliefs and morals. The new demonic religion was called Judaism, and believers were called Jews.[22]

Having three different meanings for the term "Jew" allows Identity adherents to choose the denotation that supports their two-seed theory; the term always seems to mean something other than what the "outsider" thinks.

The meaning of the word "Gentile" is also twisted for Identity purposes. Identity adherents argue that it is either a satanic ploy or a lie spread by ignorant "Judeo-Christian" apostate teachers that the apostle Paul and others went out to give the gospel of Jesus Christ to nonwhites. In the biblical account of the apostle Paul's encounter with Jesus on the road to Damascus, Jesus told Paul, "I will send you far away to the Gentiles" (Acts 22:21; see also Acts 9:15). Thus Christians teach that the apostle Paul was to preach the gospel among non-Jews. But, according to Identity's circular reasoning, if Jesus was sent only to white Israel, then it cannot be true that Paul was sent to any people except white Israelites. That Paul was sent to the Gentiles must mean that "Gentiles" is a reference to white Israelites in dispersion among other races and in other nations. The Greek word for Gentile is *ethnos*, commonly translated "nation" or "people," and is the most general term denoting the natural, loose cohesion of people. This can include people in contrast to the king, every nation of humankind, or non-Jewish Gentiles in contrast to Jews.[23] But in Identity theology, the claim is that the Greek word *ethnos* stands for "race" or "tribe." Jesus' instructions to Paul are taken as meaning that Paul did not go to other races but "spent his entire ministry preaching to the White Race."[24] In this

light, all of the letters of the Christian Scriptures are addressed to
and belong to the white race.

JESUS' MISSION TO WHITE ISRAEL

Two areas of study for Christian theologians are Christology, the theological interpretation of the person and work of Christ, and Soteriol-
ogy, theology dealing with salvation, especially as brought about by
Christ. Identity's view of the person and work of Christ is rooted in
God's special creation and election of the white race. What Identity
theology calls the Law of Kinsman Redemption specifies that Jesus can
redeem only those of the Adamic (white) seed. Why? Because it is this
seed-line that God entered when God became human.[25]

What about reaching out to the other races? According to
Identity, such work is not needed. All races other than whites are outside the realm of Jesus' redemptive work. The truth for Identity is
that the "Seed of the Serpent cannot be saved."[26] The majority of the
world cannot know God because they have been "inbred with the personality of Satan . . . the door of salvation is closed to Satan's Seed."[27]

Jesus' incarnation in the seed of Adam is vital to Identity's sote-
riology; his genes and skin color are indispensable to their doctrine
concerning salvation.[28] Jesus Christ came in the role of the "'Kinsman Redeemer' to save the people whose nature and physical seed
he possessed. . . . This dynamic announcement will cancel most of
the evangelical ideas about Christ coming to save all peoples of the
earth. Jesus Christ came as a kinsman redeemer to save the people
whose seed he embraced."[29]

What is the purpose of ministry? For Identity the continuing
power of the preaching and teaching of Jesus' words is that they sift
"the wheat and the weeds," separating the chosen race from among
Jews and mixed bloods. Jesus' words regarding his ministry in the
Gospel of Matthew and his instructions to his disciples on their first
evangelistic journey are taken as proof of his partiality for the white
race. Jesus said, "I was sent *only* to the lost sheep of the house of
Israel" (Matt. 15:24; see also Matt. 10:5–6).[30] The disciples' mission
to the elect would take them *only* to the fair-skinned Israelites of all
the nations, a call going out to the white race to awaken them from
their racial slumber, remember their election as the chosen people,
and come out from among the seed of the serpent and the colored
"beasts of the field" in order to live out their blessed destiny.

Thus Jesus is made the segregationist supreme, calling the
white race to pursue racial purity and "build an Ark of Safety" for

the race.[31] The urgency of the racial Jesus' call for segregation undergirds Aryan Nations' "Platform for the Aryan National State," which calls for annexing a geographical area where "only Aryans (white race) are allowed citizenship."[32] The call for purity of the race as a way of practicing one's faith also undergirds the larger movement, "the Northwest Imperative," which has attracted growing numbers of white separatists to the northwest United States with the ultimate goal of annexing all or a portion of North America for an Aryan homeland.[33]

Along with Jesus' saving significance for the white race, specific details of his life, teaching, and preaching are interpreted through the Identity lens. For example, in the Gospel of Matthew, when Jesus reminds his listeners that the God he reveals is "the God of Abraham, the God of Isaac, and the God of Jacob" (Matt. 22:32), Identity devotees claim that Jesus is referring to the genealogy of the white race.[34] In another instance, the devil was able to tempt Jesus during his forty days in the wilderness with authority over "all the kingdoms of the world" (Luke 4:5) because Satan, through his offspring the Jews, had taken control of all human-made kingdoms and governments, kept the white race ignorant of their true identity, and lowered their spiritual stature through race mixing.[35] And when on the Mount of Transfiguration Jesus' clothes become "dazzling white" in the divine glow of his calling as Son of God (Matt. 17:2), and the angels that appear at Jesus' tomb to announce his resurrection are described as wearing "clothing white as snow" (Matt. 28:3), these colors used to point to Jesus' divine origins and position as God's Son, Identity adherents argue, prove that God's preference is for the color white.[36]

God's preference for the white race even "colors" the interpretation of texts that seem to reveal Jesus' love and mercy for outsiders such as Samaritans. When Jesus interacted with the Samaritan woman at the well (John 4:1–42), that this woman came to faith in Jesus was proof that she must have been an Israelite: "Her response of faith could not be the response of a Jew; neither is it the response of the heathen . . . it is the response of an Israelite! . . . And in this meeting she is symbolic of all Israel meeting Christ their Messiah."[37] For Identity adherents, Jesus is a type of Aryan warrior who has come to do battle with the forces of evil incarnate from Satan's seed-line. Jesus is engaged in a racial battle, calling the white race to wake up concerning their true identity and calling the offspring of Satan children of the devil (John 8:44) so that they might be identified and treated, which in some Identity circles means extermination. The Identity

Jesus calls the white race to "come out" of Babylon (Rev. 18:4), the world corrupted by Satan's offspring, and be a separated people.[38] This "coming out" will not be without cost, however, because Satan is doing relentless battle in an attempt to authenticate Satan's counterfeit seed-line. Their Jesus was crucified by the satanic Jews. And white Israelites who know their true identity should expect to be persecuted during the battle for the preservation of their race. During the Montana Freemen's standoff in Jordan, the Freemen quoted Jesus' Sermon on the Mount as a word for their comfort: "Blessed are those persecuted for righteousness' sake, for theirs is the kingdom of heaven. Blessed are you when men revile you and persecute you and utter all kinds of evil against you falsely on my account (Matt. 5:10–12)."[39] And brothers and sisters of the racial faith believed that the Montana Freemen were being "held hostage" and "forced to submit to Satan."[40]

THE EARLY MISSION OF THE CHRISTIAN CHURCH

In the Identity view, God has sent Jesus Christ to save the white race; the other races will never enter the kingdom of God. Geographically speaking, this shifts the initial missionary journeys of the first-century disciples to northwest Europe:

> The history of Europe after Christ is of the fulfilling of Christ's prophetic pronouncements on His "lost sheep" as the Anglo-Saxon, Celtic, Germanic, and Scandinavian people were converted to Christ almost as fast as the Word could be carried to them. They heard His voice, and they followed Him. Within a few hundred years, every King in Europe was crowned as a sovereign in the Name of the Lord.[41]

The Bible reveals that the apostle Paul had plans to travel to Spain. However, there is no biblical evidence that Paul ever made that journey. It is likely that perhaps four to six years after Paul wrote his letter to the Romans, he was executed by Roman authorities. Speaking of his collection of offerings from Christian churches to be distributed among the people in need in the Jerusalem church, Paul wrote to the church in Rome, "Now, with no further place for me in these regions, I desire, as I have for many years, to come to you when I go to Spain" (Rom. 15:23–24; see 15:28). Some Identity adherents claim that Paul's desire to go to Spain materialized; they cite a lost chapter of the book of Acts that gives the account of Paul's journey to Spain and then on to the British Isles, where he helped establish the first Christian churches.[42]

> And no man hindered Paul, for he had testified boldly of Jesus before tribunes, and among the people, and they took shipping at Ostium, and having winds fair, were brought safely into a haven of Spain. And much people were gathered together from the towns and villages and the hill country; for they had heard of the conversion of the Apostle, and the many miracles which he had wrought. And Paul preached mightily in Spain, and great multitudes believed and were converted, for they perceived he was an Apostle sent from God. (Lost Chapter, vv. 4–6)[42]

By the response Paul purportedly received in Spain, it is assumed that those who greeted him must have been white Israelites who had made their way to Spain during the Babylonian exile of Judah in 587 B.C.E.[44] "Paul and the Word received an enthusiastic welcome in Spain. This was not the cold hatred of the 'Jews' for the Gospel, neither was it the curious indifference of the heathen. THIS WAS THE WELCOME OF ISRAELITES!"[45] This same circular reasoning is used concerning Philip's encounter with the Ethiopian eunuch (Acts 8:26–40). Though "many claim that this is the story of the conversion of a black man," the fact that the eunuch listened to Philip's exposition of the scriptures and responded in such a positive fashion "would tend to suggest that he was, in fact, one of the lost sheep of the house of Israel," in other words, a white man.[46] Also among the claimed neglected and hidden "facts" of the history of the early Christian church is that Timothy (Rom. 16:21; 1 Cor. 4:17), a frequent companion and emissary for the apostle Paul, baptized his own nephew, the British king Lucius, who in turn declared all of England as Christian in 156 C.E.: "The first nation that proclaimed [Christianity] as their religion and called it Christian after the name of Christ was Britain."[47]

Paul's were not the only journeys to the dispersed Israelites in northern Europe that Identity remembers; Joseph of Arimathea also traveled there as early as 36–39 C.E.[48] Although the little we know about Joseph of Arimathea is given in the Bible in conjunction with Jesus' crucifixion and burial (Matt. 27:57), Identity adherents fill out his history and conclude that he was close kin to Jesus, was personally known by Pilate and the Roman soldiery, and

was a secret convert to Christ who became "one of the most effective and beloved teachers of 'the Way.'"[49] Just after the death and
resurrection of Jesus Christ, Joseph is claimed to have traveled to
present-day France to preach the gospel, having as traveling companions other biblical figures such as Martha (John 11:5), Mary
Magdalene (Matt. 27:56), Lazarus, whom Jesus raised from the
dead (John 12:1), Simon the Zealot, Zacchaeus, Paul, Peter, and
Philip, all of whom left Jerusalem about 35 C.E.[50]

> The Apostle Paul, Joseph of Arimathea, and others who
> knew their Lord "in the flesh," carried the Gospel of Jesus
> Christ to the Western part of Europe and the British Isles
> shortly after the death and Resurrection of Jesus. They
> established churches there and began the preaching that
> Christianized Western Europe and set the stage for
> England and Ireland to become the early Christian and
> missionary centers of the world.[51]

It is claimed that Joseph of Arimathea was the religious leader of this
band of Christians. His descendants became the religious and civil
leaders of the British Isles, and among his descendants are King
Arthur, the Knights of the Round Table, and the present queen of
England. The Druids of ancient Britain fit into the fanciful Identity
scheme neatly; they have been victims of the Roman Catholic
Church's false doctrine and lies. For example, though the book *St.
Paul in Britain* was written in the nineteenth century by a British
pastor asserting apostolic precedence over the church of Rome, this
work is co-opted by Identity adherents. In this work the Druids and
British citizens are described as the great patriots of the past, pos-
sessing superior minds, exceptional reverence for the law, bravery,
and desire for freedom. In the face of expanding Roman imperialism
they were the only true freemen. Identity claims that the Druids were
no pagans; their racial lineage could be traced back to fifty years after
the birth of Adam's son Seth (Gen. 4:25). Druidism was brought into
Britain by a contemporary of the biblical patriarch Abraham, and
living among the Druids were Hebrews of the lost tribes. And,
Identity asserts, before the Christian missionaries arrived, the Druids
already taught the coming of the Messiah, the doctrine of the Trinity,
and vicarious atonement. To Identity, the Druids were a vital and
indispensable part of the Christian missionary work in Britain:
"Nowhere, then, in Asia, Africa, or Europe, could the apostles find
richer or a better prepared soil for the Gospel."[52] For them, there was

never a time "when the Druids of Britain held not to its doctrines."[53] By claiming that Paul and Joseph of Arimathea traveled to Spain and northwest Europe, Identity adherents have transplanted the land from which Christianity arose from the shores of Galilee and Asia Minor to northwest Europe.

THE SEED OF ADAM TODAY

Today only a remnant of the seed of Adam has had its "blindness" lifted and has realized its identity as the true Israel.[54] But this remnant does not include those who remain faithful to the Torah or those who believe in God's justifying forgiveness and reconciliation given in Jesus Christ. This remnant includes those who "know" they are members of God's chosen seed-line, the Adamic white race, and believe that Jesus came to save that seed-line. This eclectic remnant is made up of "believers" who attend the growing number of Identity congregations throughout the country and the world. It includes the Constitutional vanguards fighting for the rights of "organic citizenship" and a return to "God's laws." It includes the front-line warriors adhering to the violent goals and means of the Phineas Priesthood (see chapter 8), and those among the current rise in militias warding off the satanic, Jew-controlled federal government and training for battle, or fighting to annex a part or all of the United States and create an Aryan republic.

For many of these new racial extremists, the United States is literally "that great nation promised to the seed of Abraham, Isaac, and Jacob"; the United States is literally the "birthright nation" bequeathed to Joseph's son Manasseh (Gen. 48); the United States is literally "the New Jerusalem" and the "land of the regathering" of the lost tribes of Israel comprised of "the Anglo-Saxon, Celtic, German, Scandinavian and Kindred peoples of the world."[55] While many Identity disciples think that "Ephraim-Israel will chiefly be found" in the British Isles, others assert that it was no mere accident that the United States had thirteen originating colonies representing the "completeness of the tribes of Israel."[56] The work *America: Zion of God* lists "fifteen reasons why America is the Zion of God,"[57] several of which are listed here:

- The tide of immigrations that took place prior to and with the formation of the United States is thought to fulfill the prophecy that God's people would be "gathered from many nations" (Ezek. 38:8).

- The colonial expansion west from the Atlantic is claimed to have been prophesied: "Thy waste and thy desolate places . . . shall even now be too narrow by reason of the inhabitants. . . . The children which thou shalt have . . . shall say again in thine ears, 'The place is too straight for me: give place to me that I may dwell'" (Isa. 49:19–20 KJV).[58]
- The United States is thought to be "the land shadowing with wings, which is beyond the rivers of Ethiopia" (Isa. 18:1 KJV) since, as one Identity author puts it, "you will find no other land or people on that line of latitude until you strike the United States of America." Also, that the prophesied land would be one "shadowing with wings" is taken as a prophecy of one of the U.S. national symbols, the eagle with outstretched wings.

The apocalyptic potency of Identity theology fed by this religio-mystical nationalism dictates that the United States will be one of the hubs of "the kingdom age," which is "about to burst upon us."[59]

THE FUTURE OF THE SEED OF ADAM

Though the hour is late, and the process of degeneracy well-advanced, it is NOT TOO LATE for the remaining Aryan men and women to form a community, an ethnic state and, eventually, a NEW NATION.[60]

As the world moves ever onward to the end times, it is of critical importance that Israel should finally wake up from its "sleep of death," realize its biblical identity, and engage in battle with the enemy to preserve the white race.[61] For Identity, the fundamental obstacle to the continued fulfillment of the prophetic role of Israel has to do with apathetic and dull white Israelites unaware of their racial identity: "In the final days of this closing age, as all the heathen and anti-Christ forces of the world are gathered against the Saxon-Israel Race, there is no other knowledge that will remove the smokescreen of ignorance and propaganda that surrounds us, like the knowledge of our identity as God's Chosen Race."[62]

In looking to the future, the specter portended by Identity visionaries is one not only of white Israel's triumph but for some, an eventual racial apocalypse and the extermination of the enemies of God's people. Identity speculations shift the epicenter of the most significant action, the primary theater for their tribulation and racial holy war, from Palestine and the Middle East toward the United

States. Those who believe the United States is, in effect, biblical Israel see events in the Middle East as preliminary, perhaps a distraction, for what will be the main battle center, North America. The consummating struggle will pit the personification of cosmic evil and children of Satan, the Jews, against Aryans. Related to this, Identity extremism is suspicious of any kind of rapture doctrine that allows for the escape of the elect before the racial apocalypse, and it is belligerent about the philo-Semitism endemic in Christian fundamentalists' dispensational doctrine that calls for the Jews to be restored to their homeland before the prophetic clock again begins to move forward. The rapture doctrine, it is argued, is a "Jewish fable" that leads to apathy, a kind of apocalyptic sleep among white Israel, who in fact should be preparing for war: "There is a terrible time of trouble coming upon us my Kinsmen. . . . We do know that there will be no 'rapture.' WE ARE HIS WEAPONS AND BATTLE AXES OF WAR!"[63]

While some of the new racial extremists take a more disengaging stance toward the world, others view the onrush of the end times as a challenge to be faced with weapons and paramilitary training. They take this preparation very seriously because the power and pervasiveness of the enemy are almost overwhelming. Because of the tendency toward a pure incarnational dualism, and the power and continuing spread of the seed of the serpent, an oscillation between pessimism and resignation, on the one hand, and the call to battle with triumphalistic confidence, on the other hand, are common in Identity circles. What if there are not enough faithful white soldiers? As the world approaches the "Kingdom Age," a racial apocalyptic battle and the greatest tribulation known to the Adamic race loom large. Communities and families are encouraged to strive for self-sufficiency and prepare a geographic refuge. The ultimate disaster is not natural but demographic, related to a fear that the tribulation may result in the destruction of the white race.

With Identity's incarnational dualism the threat to God's salvific purposes resides in the blood, and the "final solution" involves the spilling of blood and the obliteration of Satan's kids from the face of the earth—whether at the hands of revolutionary millennialists or an enraged racial deity. And unless historical events give cause for significant doctrinal mutations (known to Identity theology), the near future in the United States and other bastions of racial extremism will continue to include the urgent need to expose the cosmic crime of the stolen birthright and preparation for war until there is "One Aryan nation, under God."[64]

4

THE PERSECUTION
COMPLEX OF WHINERS

*A favorite ploy of the Seed of the Serpent is to amalgamate
with the Seed of Adam.*

—Dan Gayman[1]

For Identity adherents, the seed of Adam has left its mark on
the world stage, God's chosen white race in dispersion. But so
has the despicable seed of the serpent left its mark through its
characteristic genetic constitution, shape and size, propensities
toward murder and deceit, and a "conspiracy for power that
extends into every dimension of life."[2] Tracing the serpent's seed is
an indispensable endeavor for Identity's conspiracy theorists.

A HISTORY OF FALSE CLAIMS AND WHINING

According to the claims of Identity, Satan fathered the literal child,
Cain, by means of Eve. Abel was the child of Adam and Eve. Cain
killed his half brother, Abel, because Cain became murderously
jealous when God accepted Abel's sacrifice. After being marked for
this murder, Cain left the Garden of Eden to dwell among the inferior pre-Adamic people of color (Gen. 4:16).

Outside of Eden Cain and his descendants continued to wreak
havoc on the seed of Adam. The enmity spoken of in Genesis 3:15
was destined to continue, Identity adherents assert, as the seed of

the serpent, with all their evil intent, continued to live in close prox-imity to the seed of Adam. After the Flood, Identity claims that the serpent's trail can be traced through the characteristics of self-pity, murder, and deceit first displayed by Cain (Gen. 4:4–5).

"A persecution complex has been a fixed trait with the seed of the serpent throughout their history. They dote on telling others about their misfortunes, going to any extreme to keep records of their persecution and afflictions."[3] Because of this persecution complex, Identity asserts that persecution of Jews and a Jewish Holocaust are a hoax, a "completely mythical"[4] fabrication of the seed of the serpent used to elicit sympathy.

To trace the seed of the serpent in all of their deceptive guises, Identity extremism draws upon revisionist organizations and indi-vidual "scholars" at work to "expose" what they call the "holocaust myth." The claim is that Cain's persecution complex, which runs through the Jews' desire to elicit sympathy, created Holocaust "post-war propaganda," which is in fact a "colossal piece of fiction"[5] used "to extort money, exert privilege, extort political advantage, and exert moral superiority."[6] Holocaust denial material is welcomed from organizations such as the Institute for Historical Review[7] and the Committee for Open Debate on the Holocaust[8] as well as from individuals, including the Canadian neo-Nazi Ernst Zundel, whose publishing firm released the first Canadian edition (1980) of *Did Six Million Really Die?*[9] According to Zundel's Internet site, Zundelsite, the book has since been circulated in eighteen coun-tries and twelve languages. Holocaust denial enterprises aim to "reshape history in order to rehabilitate the persecutors and demo-nize the victims."[10] Drawing on a well of pseudohistory that began in the United States following World War II, they have been active worldwide in England, France, Belgium, Austria, Australia, New Zealand, Argentina, Mexico, Chile, Peru, and Japan.

Deniers have had more than a little help from leaders of the Arab world, some of whom scorn "the lie about six million Jews who were murdered." Some Arabs have gone one step further with their "inversion of history," spreading lies concerning Zionism's self-interested and friendly dealings with the Nazis; they have accused Zionist Jews of sending other Jews to the gas chambers in order to secure their own *Lebensraum* (living space) in the Middle East.[11]

Deniers have long engaged in what has been called an "inces-tuous merry-go-round [of] cross-fertilizing and compounding [of] falsehood."[12] Not given to subtleties or afraid of revisionist over-statements, the new racial extremists tend to claim that only white

Israel has been persecuted over the centuries: "From the day of John the Baptist until now, white Christians alone, not the Jews, have suffered severe persecutions."[13]

Holocaust denial begins with the seemingly innocent charge that all war is evil and that no one side can be blamed. The next move is to claim that the atrocities committed by the Allies on German troops and citizens far outweighed those perpetrated by the Germans, and that, as a result, any evident German anti-Semitism, however little, was defensive. On the tail of these are claims that accusations concerning the murder of six million Jews are a gross exaggeration based on forged and planted documents and forced, distorted, or mistaken testimony. These claims are backed up by pseudoscientific and pseudohistorical data refuting the possibility of the extermination of so many people and denying the existence of death camps, gas chambers, and any intention to harm "innocent" Jews. All the while, as the decades passed, the arguments and statistical claims became more sophisticated and complicated. Given the strong ties between Holocaust deniers and Identity extremists, one should expect Holocaust denial rhetoric to continue where Identity exists and Cain's descendants are being ferreted out.

In the biblical narrative, Cain's punishment for killing his brother, Abel, was that he would be "a fugitive and a wanderer on the earth" (Gen. 4:12). Identity adherents charge, as many throughout the centuries, that the Jews are wandering parasites who, without a homeland of their own, are continuously looking for host nations to feed upon. And as Cain's offspring multiplied and spread abroad, so did the conspiracy against the seed of Adam and God's plans for the white race. Throughout history, the seed of the serpent have been able to gain the upper hand financially and politically because they do not live by the morals of the seed of Adam. A world perceived as filled with the proliferation of the satanic offspring of Cain is seen clearly in the wide-sweeping conspiracy theories constructed by the new racial extremists.

THE SEED OF THE SERPENT IN THE PROMISED LAND

Identity claims that the serpent seduced Eve in the garden and spread its seed through Cain's offspring, who survived the Flood and first manifested themselves in the people of Canaan, since "this wicked seed-line preceded Abraham into the promised land."[14] By the time of Abraham the seed of the serpent were well established in Canaan, the new racial extremists insist. Satan's agenda was to replace true Israel with his seed-line and ultimately to pass off one of his own kids as messiah of the world. Through their satanic culture the Canaanites were among the originators and practitioners of black magic, devil worship, witchcraft, incest, adultery, and bestiality.

The Bible records that Abraham and Sarah had a son, Isaac, who was to be the bearer of the promises of God (Gen. 21:1–3). In turn Isaac had two sons, Jacob and Esau (Gen. 25:24–26). And even before the Adamic white race entered into the promised land in sustained and concentrated proximity to the serpent seed, Esau married into the foreign Hittite tribe (Gen. 26:34–35), claimed by Identity to be a tribe of the Canaanite branch of the serpent seed. Through this mixed marriage the seed of the serpent would be perpetuated through Esau's offspring: "A favorite ploy of the Seed of the Serpent is to amalgamate with the Seed of Adam. The marriage of Esau into the Hittite/Canaanite bloodline provided a genetic linkup for the descendants of Esau (also known as Edom; Gen. 36:8) to take on the corrupt nature and character of the Seed of the Serpent."[15] As a result of this satanic race mixing, there have been genetic intrusions by Satan into the Adamic race's seed-line. And because Satan's children were fathered by the likes of Esau, Judah, and Simeon, there has always been a time when the seed of the serpent could deceptively claim descent from Abraham by way of the father and these "out of kind" marriages.

Identity doctrine traces virtually every adversary of biblical Israel to the seed of the serpent: the Canaanites, the Edomites, the Ammonites, the Amalekites, the Hittites, the Amorites, the Perizzites, the Moabites, the Jebusites, the Hivites, and the Girgashites. And Esau's descendants, Identity adherents claim, became one of the most wicked branches of Satan's children, with effects on the seed of Adam reverberating even into the history of the Christian Scriptures. For example, one claim is that King Herod was from the wicked Edomite seed-line and was out to displace the seed of Adam when he ordered the murder of all white male children living in Jerusalem at the time of Jesus' birth (Matt. 2:16–17).[16] The seed of the serpent, the Canaanites and their kinsmen, surrounded the Israelites in the promised land. Identity claims that this ability of Satan's children to successfully race mix explains why in the Christian Scriptures the Pharisees could say to Jesus, "We are descendants of Abraham" (John 8:33).[17] But, the new racial extremists claim, "a little bit of Canaanite blood spoils the whole lump."[18] The ever-present danger was the serpent seed's desire to incarnate themselves in the Adamic race, alluring the Israelites to race mix for the purposes of aborting God's plans of incarnating in the seed of Adam through Jesus Christ.

As Moses led the people Israel to the brink of the promised land, he gave instructions from God forbidding interaction between Israel and the other nations (Deut. 7:1–3). For the new racial extremists, the danger was not the allure of the gods of the Canaanites and other neighbors, but the danger of race mixing with Satan's offspring. Under the leadership of Joshua, the Israelite armies conquered Canaan. According to Identity adherents, those who were killed were of the seed of the serpent and, because of their genetic makeup, should have been completely eradicated. But many Canaanites were allowed to live and continued to work on Satan's behalf to snare and scourge the seed of Adam. During the reign of the judges of Israel, the intermittent wars between the Israelites and surrounding nations are taken as proof of the continued enmity spoken of in Genesis 3:15. Under the leadership of the judges, the Adamic race continued to wage the age-old warfare against the seed of the serpent, who continued to dwell in the land; the book of Judges was a "detailed account" of this warfare. This enmity continued to be recorded throughout First and Second Kings and First and Second Chronicles. The seed of the serpent constantly plagued white Israel.

The Bible records that Israel and Judah were exiled from the land given by God following defeat by the military powers of Assyria and Babylon, respectively. Identity writers assert that while in Babylonian captivity the people of the southern two-tribed Judah did not maintain their racial integrity. The serpent's seed made successful intrusions into Adam's seed-line once again. For Identity adherents this is a formational time in tracing the tracks of Satan's kids on the world stage; many of the Edomite and Canaanite people already in Babylon became subversive proselytes.[19] The changes that took place within Judaism as a result of the Exile are taken as proof of satanic influences on Israel's culture and religion; Judaism became the religion of "Israel's ancient pagan enemy."[20] The Pentateuch (the first five books of the Bible) is said to have been abandoned by these people for the Babylonian Talmud, "the very heart and soul of the Serpent race."[21] The synagogue, generally speaking, replaced Jerusalem Temple worship, and the prophets and priests became rabbis and scribes. The new racial extremists today warn that the satanic dangers of Judaism must be avoided, even eradicated. The inroads Satan's kids have been able to forge even into the church result in what Identity devotees scornfully call

Judeo-Christianity. Any kind of connection drawn between "true" Christianity and Judaism is the work of the serpent's seed. Israel must work to "set people free from the dreadful and soul-destroying ideology behind Judeo-Christianity"[22] designed to bring in a godless new age with a new morality based on secular humanism.

THE SEED OF THE SERPENT
IN THE CHRISTIAN SCRIPTURES

In the Christian Scriptures, Identity thinkers trace the seed of the serpent through the speech and actions of the Jews, Pharisees, Sadducees, and scribes. The polemics of Jesus and his disciples against those who did not believe Jesus was the Christ are taken as proof that "the Serpent Seed dominated both the Pharisees and the Sadducees at this point in history."[23] The Pharisees and scribes who did not believe in Jesus as the Christ could not believe, Identity claims, because they were not white Israelites; they were of satanic origins. And the age-old enmity prophesied in Genesis 3:15 is played out in the Gospels of the Christian Scriptures until ulti-mately the serpent's seed committed the unforgivable crime of deicide, the murder of Jesus Christ. Keeping in mind the theory of the two seed-lines and surveying some of the polemics from the Christian Scriptures, one can imagine Identity's co-option of the texts. When he saw some Pharisees and Sadducees approaching, John the Baptist trumpeted, "You brood of vipers!" (Matt. 3:7–9). Though in the same breath John called them to repentance, that they were called vipers is taken as proof of their literal satanic origins and the "ultimate damnation of the Serpent Seed."[24] In another place, Jesus' warning concerning false prophets who come "in sheep's clothing but inwardly are ravenous wolves," represents to the new racial extremists Satan's offspring who try to pass them-selves off as God's chosen race and are out to destroy God's true sheep, white Israel (Matt. 7:15–20). Likewise, Jesus' parable of the wheat and the weeds (Matt. 13:24–30) is said to describe the infil-tration of the seed of the serpent whose "purpose it is to destroy God's Israel!"[25] The deceitful advancement of the theology and agenda of the seed of the serpent is thought to be compared by Jesus to yeast in bread when he warned, "Beware of the yeast of the Pharisees and Sadducees!" (Matt. 16:5–11). When Jesus confronted some scribes and Pharisees and called them snakes and a brood of vipers (Matt. 23:33), Jesus was exposing the Jews as "literally a race of snakes . . . the Serpent Seed."[26]

Using Identity's interpretive lens to trace the seed of the serpent beyond the Gospels, we see in the book of Acts that the apostle Paul called a sorcerer named Elymas a "son of the devil." One can predict that Identity takes this as proof that Elymas was a literal descendant of Satan (Acts 13:10). And Paul's polemical language directed toward his kinsmen is again taken as proof of expression of the ceaseless enmity between the seed of Adam and the seed of the serpent when he is paraphrased as declaring, "Jews killed the Lord Jesus Christ, the Prophets, have persecuted us, please not God, and are CONTRARY TO ALL MEN!"[27] Identity's version of the revelation given to John the Seer substantiates this view when he exposed the Jews as the "synagogue of Satan" (Rev. 2:9),[28] the place of worship for Satan's kids.

The most diabolical act of the seed of the serpent in the Christian Scriptures was the murder of Jesus. Wesley Swift, in the book *Reopening the Trial of Jesus Christ*,[29] claims that while the Pharisees "believed many deep truths" including the special "sovereignty of the white race," the Sadducees were made up of "a part of the Luciferian descendancy" who had "attached themselves" to positions of influence. The result of this interpretation is that Jesus' trial and death are perceived as a successful conspiratorial plot by a branch of the seed of the serpent, the Sanhedrin of Jerusalem, a council of Jewish leaders taken over by Sadducees passing themselves off as Pharisees so that they could possess the majority of the seats on the council for Satan's political and theological advantage. At the time of Jesus, Swift argues, the Temple was dominated by satanic Canaanite priests, and wherever there is reference to animosities or plots against Jesus, these wicked Canaanite priests and their devotees are the perpetrators. As Swift weaves the tale, despite Gamaliel's and Nicodemus's valiant efforts, the Jews—the Sadducees—condemned Jesus to death. Swift exonerates Pontius Pilate and the Roman government of any complicity in Jesus' death. Pilate is described as born in Spain "of a rather high family" and educated in Druid universities in London; he was "a white man of the tribe of Simeon," whether he knew it or not. Because of his genetic makeup and lineage, he could not have killed Jesus. As a sign of this, Swift claims, when Pilate washed his hands (Matt. 27:24), he effectively became innocent of any complicity in Jesus' death. In contrast, any ill that has fallen upon the present-day Jews throughout the centuries "has not been persecution, but retribution"[30] for their involvement in Jesus' death.

Sheldon Emry, in *Who Killed Christ?*, conducts his study in the form of a pseudo-investigation of a murder.[31] For Emry, there are no distinctions; the Pharisees, elders, Sadducees, scribes, and chief priests were all of a "race of people eternally hostile to true Israel."[32] In Emry's work, Pilate is completely exonerated of any complicity in Jesus' death. First, the Jews, who knew how to use their power ruthlessly, "set about to FORCE Pilate to give his consent for them to put Jesus Christ to death." Second, in Emry's tale, Pilate made "almost desperate attempts" to save Jesus from death. And, consistent with Swift's story, Emry claims that Pilate underwent an ancient Israelite ritual of absolution before the satanic Jews took Jesus into their own hands to crucify him.[33] In a creative twist Emry proceeds to evacuate nearly every Roman soldier from the events surrounding Jesus' suffering and crucifixion so that all who remain are the "wicked Jews" who must have killed him. In the Gospel of Matthew's account of the events surrounding Jesus' trial and crucifixion, after we are told that "the soldiers of the governor took Jesus into the governor's headquarters" (Matt. 27:27), Emry contends that the soldiers turned Jesus over to the chief priests and Pharisees; from that point, the soldiers had nothing to do with Jesus' mocking, suffering, and death. And, he adds, this reading is substantiated by the Gospels of Mark, Luke, and John.[34] Emry's conclusion: the seed of the serpent killed Jesus in their relentless battle to thwart God's plans and pass themselves off as the chosen race.[35]

SATAN'S KIDS IN DISPERSION

Identity theorists claim that after the destruction of the Temple of Jerusalem (70 C.E.), the Jews fled the city, and this dispersion of the seed of the serpent quickly became the merchants, bankers, traders, usurers, and power behind the throne of governments throughout the world positioned strategically to fulfill "their unique role as the catalyst and engine of destruction and the decomposition and death of every culture or civilization the Aryan ever creates."[36] After the destruction of the Temple, Satan's kids residing in the area are claimed to have divided into two main branches: the Sephardim, who dispersed themselves northwest into Spain and beyond, and the Ashkenazim, who are more easily tracked and moved into what is now Eastern Europe and parts of Russia in order to build a worldwide satanic kingdom. From the Ashkenazim, they claim, arose the Khazar Empire, "the next major concentration of Serpent Seed,"[37] a mixture of Canaanites, Edomites, and other branches of Satan's offspring who infiltrated the Mongols and Turks; this Khazarian kingdom lasted until approximately 1000 C.E., at which time the

Russians conquered it. Next, Identity history concludes that the wicked Khazarians, who had come to embrace the satanic cult Judaism, moved in large numbers into Poland, Russia, and other Eastern European countries. The millions of the serpent seed living in these countries became the population pool from which Eastern European Jewry arose and were the Jews whom Hitler valiantly battled.[38] In the late 1800s and early 1900s these Ashkenazim serpent seed made their way by the tens of thousands to the United States to feed on another host country, which was bequeathed to white Israel for a homeland: "For the past two millenniums this Serpent Seed has attacked the foundations of every Christian state on earth and has waged an eternal warfare with the Seed of [Adam]."[39]

In the United States, "the seat of International Jewish power,"[40] the new racial extremists believe they are engaged in a racial holy war with the serpent seed, the Canaanites who have now come to Israel's promised land to defile it with drugs developed in Jewish laboratories, liquor, gambling, humanism, revolutionary literature, sexual perversions, and race mixing:[41] "[The Jews] have infiltrated our schools, the news media, even churches and government in their attempt to keep you in ignorance of your identity as Israelites. They are attempting to steal your heritage that they may conquer America and take rule over the whole earth."[42] In the United States, Identity accuses, Jews promote abortion and abortion clinics in order to destroy white babies: "The abortion clinics, which have murdered nearly 15 million White babies in the last ten years, are almost exclusively Jewish."[43] And through the Jews, one of the "greatest hoaxes ever perpetrated on an unsuspecting people"[44] is disseminated, the doctrine of human equality: "We Believe . . . the Jew is like a destroying virus that attacks our racial body to destroy our White culture and purity of our Race."[45] The Montana Freemen were not simply protesting government corruption; they believed they were battling these evil invaders, including the "agents of 'Satan' in congress of today," who are likened to "the four hundred and fifty prophets of Baal"[46] whom the prophet Elijah faced on Mount Carmel (1 Kings 18).

Throughout the history of hostility with the Adamic white race, Satan's offspring have left a trail of blood. They have been the cause and supporters of wars, insurrections, and revolutions in countless nations including World War I, World War II, the American Civil War, and the French and Russian Revolutions. The children of Adam "have been sent into the battlefields to die"[47] in order to weaken the seed of Adam. To control the outcome of every divisive event "ALWAYS the Jew runs both sides of every divided faction"; their ultimate goal is "to subvert and destroy Christianity, and ultimately the entire Aryan race."[48]

From this point, the task of tracing the seed of the serpent and the battle between the children of light and the children of darkness—whether in the guise of the United Nations and the threat of a one-world government, anti-gun legislation, the world bankers, the federal government, the NAACP, the Masons, the media, the IRS, the New Age movement, the Vatican, the World Council of Churches, and more—takes us into the strange and threatening world of contemporary conspiracy theories.[49] For Identity adherents, at the root of the conspiracies is the serpent's seed. Conspirators and Identity believers cross paths here. Identity adherents may refer to and sell books, tapes, and videos that may not explicitly espouse Identity doctrine, such as *None Dare Call It Conspiracy*.[50] The warning is sounded by conspiracy theorists that all things are being positioned for takeover by a satanic New World Order including markers on the backs of road signs to guide invading foreign troops, black helicopters doing reconnaissance on patriots and other subversives and awaiting the signal to take resisters to U.S. concentration camps,[51] and weather control for crop and, in turn, population control.[52] Identity has been aided by Arab conspiracy theorists represented by Jordan's representative to the United Nations who before the General Assembly in 1980 attempted to expose the Jewish conspiracy, "which controls, manipulates and exploits the rest of humanity by controlling the money and wealth of the world."[53]

Satan's children bind organizations to their agenda to take over the world and set up a Davidic dynasty, the blueprints of which are said to be revealed in *The Protocols of the Learned Elders of Zion:* "The goal of this group who worships Lucifer, the outcast from heaven, is to steal the birthright and rule the world by force in accordance with Lucifer's original plans."[54] For Identity believers, studying the fraudulent Protocols is "fundamental to knowing the worldview of the Serpent Seed" and informs the battle for preservation of white Israel. The warning goes out that the Jews "are making world revolution and war inevitable which will climax in a reign of violence and bloodshed bringing the present age to its close."[55] The wide-sweeping occupation and work of the seed of the serpent that are imagined create an ever-present and spreading danger, which leads to a kind of apocalyptic aggression by Identity believers. White Israelites must awaken, arm themselves, and beware. The only reason white Israel has not heard of Satan's plot and Israel's danger is that "there has been a conspiracy of silence through a controlled mass media, controlled publishing houses, and controlled education, including religious institutions."[56]

Great Britain and the United States play a special geographical-theological role for many Identity believers. These two countries are understood as fulfilling the role of the biblical "sons of Joseph" to whom Jacob gave the birthright blessing (Gen. 48). Consistent with the goal of Satan's kids to usurp the seed of Adam from their promised homelands is the constant toil of the "Zionist occupied governments" (ZOG) of the world. The Montana Freemen maintain that Washington, D.C., is the "seat of . . . Satan," and that in their standoff with federal officials they were resisting not just a corrupt government but "Satan's servants."[57] Whatever time and place are viewed through the Identity lens, it appears that world history is being driven by a gigantic conspiracy. In fact, along with the virulent Identity theology, wide-sweeping conspiracy theories are the other ingredient of the glue that holds the new racial extremists together. These conspiracy theories are a natural outgrowth of the incarnational dualism espoused.[58] And with the relentless rise in the world population the progenies of the serpent seed are bound to grow and spread.

In Identity discussion and literature the language at times is secular, and the enemy is identified in such a way that the protagonists would probably be labeled antigovernment activists, tax protesters, or those who fall somewhere into the far right politically. But when one delves deeper into what is at the root of the conspiracy for the new racial extremists, biblical language carries the load of imagery and meaning. When one moves to what is at the root of bad government and corrupt morals, it is Satan's kids, the Jews. When these issues are explored in terms of their ramifications for the country and the world, it becomes clear that what is involved is a racial holy war, and what is at stake for the racial extremists is the survival of God's chosen white race, the true Israelites.

THE FUTURE OF THE SEED OF THE SERPENT

Identity theology asserts that, living in the last days, whites are called to combat the escalating fury of the seed of the serpent. With the Jews and their allies continuing to multiply and occupy positions of power, the cosmic conspiracy edges closer and closer to a pure dualism, the forces of darkness being almost invincible. The

Jews are a step ahead because while some of God's chosen race will
be made keenly aware of the Jews' ambitions and methods for world
domination, most of God's people remain in an apocalyptic slumber, unaware of the cosmic crime being perpetuated against their
race. According to Identity, Christian fundamentalists have fallen
for the Jewish scheme to replace God's race because they hold out
for the exalted role the Jews will play in the fulfillment of prophe-
cies in the last days. This philo-Semitic stance only aids the seed of
the serpent by freeing them from surveillance and exposure while
they continue to spread the false doctrine of the equality of all
people, take over the high places of government, control the banks,
cause wars and famine, and prepare for their desired Davidic
dynasty: "[This doctrine] has far reaching results in blinding men
to the meaning of current world developments and it has materially
assisted those who are endeavoring to acquire world rulership by
furthering their subversive activities."[59]

But, Identity believes, the racial god will continue to reveal the
identity of the conspirators who are endeavoring to enslave
humankind. And for many Identity groups this means a battle
between the seed of the serpent and the seed of Adam—a milita-
rized apocalyptic battle pitting Jew against Aryan for the survival of
the race. For many Identity adherents the focus of the main battle
theater has shifted from Palestine to the United States. Because the
enemy of the seed of the serpent is defined by blood, we are
approaching the consummation of what was prophesied in the
enmity of the two seed-lines (Gen. 3:15) and foreshadowed in the
murder of Abel (Gen. 4:8), the ruthless spilling of Aryan blood and
the coming of the "Great and Terrible Day of the Lord." Such cosmic
conspiracy theories and weapons can lead to strange behavior:
"What do you do when there are armed people in your community
who believe that a zoning ordinance is not a zoning ordinance, but
a part of a plot to take their guns, seize their land, and pack them off
to a concentration camp?"[60] Such a dualistic worldview is dangerous;
there is no sympathy for the devil. And in the Identity world there is
no future for Satan's kids. Identity's incarnational dualism will not
be relieved until Satan's kids are no longer incarnate; salvation
necessitates the extermination of the seed of the serpent.

5

FROM "JEWISH LIES"
TO *THE TURNER DIARIES*

he Hebrew and Christian Scriptures are not the only texts
shaping the racist right. Three texts that have influenced
Identity are *The Protocols of the Learned Elders of Zion*, a purported itinerary of the Jews' plan for world dominion; *The Turner
Diaries*, a work of fiction that describes a bloody racial apocalypse;
and the reformer Martin Luther's virulently anti-Judaic tract, "On
the Jews and Their Lies."

THE PROTOCOLS OF THE LEARNED ELDERS OF ZION

The Protocols of the Learned Elders of Zion is the most long-wearing and
influential work on the alleged worldwide Jewish conspiracy. This
work breeds fear concerning an invasion by the United Nations,
the New World Order, and the Zionist Occupation Government
(ZOG). Identity extremists and those who share their worldview
quote *The Protocols* as a bible for tracing the path of the seed of the
serpent and as warrant for genocide:[1] "These Protocols of the
Elders of Zion are a program for the enslavement of the world and
the destruction of Christian religion above all."[2] The following are
samples from *The Protocols*:[3]

> *Protocol 1:* Our right lies in force . . . violence must be
> the principle. . . . This evil is the one and only means to
> attain the end, the good. Therefore we must not stop at
> bribery, deceit, and treachery when they should serve the
> attainment of our end.

Protocol 10: It is indispensable to trouble in all countries the people's relations with their governments so as to utterly exhaust humanity with dissension, hatred, struggle, envy and even by the use of torture, by starvation, BY THE INOCULATION OF DISEASES, by want, so that the GOYIM see no other issue than to take refuge in our complete sovereignty. . . .

Protocol 15: When the King of Israel sets upon his sacred head the crown offered him by Europe he will become patriarch of the world.

THE BIRTH OF THE CONSPIRACY

Identity claims are particularly baffling since the Protocols were exposed as fraudulent as early as 1921, when journalist Philip Graves of the *Times* (London) proved that nearly half of them were extracted from the work of Maurice Joly, an attorney from Paris. In 1864 Joly wrote a book, *Dialogues in Hell between Machiavelli and Montesquieu, or the Politics of Machiavelli,* a satirical "thinly veiled attack on the despotism of Napoleon III [1808–73] in the form of a series of 25 dialogues," Machiavelli taking the position later associated with the Jewish conspiracy. In addition to the nearly identical pieces, the general order of Joly's work and that of the Protocols were the same.[4]

Though Joly's work directly contributed to the formulation of the Protocols, the spawning of the myth took place almost a century earlier. In 1797, in response to France's national crisis, a French cleric, Abbé Barruel, in the five-volume work *A Memoir to Serve as the History of Jacobinism,* claimed that the French Revolution was the work of the Order of Templars, a religious-military order founded during the Crusades. The Templars were brutally suppressed in France and officially dissolved by Pope Clement V in 1312. Barruel, however, claimed that some of the Templars gained control of the Freemasons and the Bavarian Illuminati and vowed to establish a worldwide republic under their control. No matter that the Freemasons and the Illuminati were rival groups and that the Illuminati was dissolved by the Bavarian government in 1786, Barruel claimed that a secret coalition of the organizations infiltrated the French government on their way to world dominion.[5] Later, Barruel was influenced by accusations against the Jews and incorporated them into his publications.[6] In such an ethos of crisis and by such seemingly haphazard means, Judeo-Masonic conspiracy theories were born.

In Germany, the development of the conspiracy was helped along with a Joly-inspired work by Herman Goedsche. Between 1866 and 1868 Goedsche wrote a series of novels, one of which contained a highly influential chapter, "In the Jewish Cemetery in Prague and the Council of Representatives of the Twelve Tribes of Israel," describing a secret meeting of Jewish leaders held every one hundred years to devise a plot for world conquest. Significantly, Goedsche's work appeared after partial German emancipation of the Jews and on the brink of their full emancipation. With the conspiracy spreading and developing, it would be during the upheaval of the Russian Revolution that the Protocols, having amalgamated sometime in the 1890s, would emerge before the public early in the 1900s.

The Jewish Conspiracy in Russia

In 1894 Tsar Nicholas II, who had taken over a highly unstable country at the age of twenty-six, came to believe that his troubles were due to the Jews, who by 1897 comprised only 4 percent of the Russian population. Sergey Nilus, a writer who had gained the favor of the imperial court, inserted a version of the Protocols into a work produced by the tsar's printing press which was used to formulate an anti-Semitic sermon to be preached in over three hundred churches in Moscow. In March 1917, Nicholas II abdicated the throne. An entry in the tsar's diary one year after he gave up the throne reveals his position regarding the Protocols: "Yesterday I started to read aloud Nilus' book on the AntiChrist, to which have been added the 'protocols' of the Jews and Masons—very timely reading."[7] Not long after that, in July 1918, Bolshevik guards murdered the imperial family.[8] Though the Jews were hated by Communist and non-Communist alike, the Bolshevik Revolution became known as part of a Jewish conspiracy, and by 1920, versions of the Protocols appeared with the warning that the Jews had destroyed the Russian Empire and murdered the imperial family, even though it was Lenin, a non-Jewish Russian, who had given the execution orders.[9]

The Spread of the Conspiracy

The history and content of the Protocols were fluid enough to allow differing conclusions about the headquarters of the conspiracy. A German, Ludwig Muller, claimed that France and England were the strongholds of the Jewish world government. Muller's version of the

Protocols was gaining popularity in Munich as Adolf Hitler was beginning his political career, and it went through thirty-three editions
before Hitler assumed power in 1933. Hitler was familiar with the
Protocols and wrote in *Mein Kampf*: "How much the whole existence
of this people is based on a permanent falsehood is proved in a
unique way by the Protocols of the Elders of Zion."[10] The Nazi Party
published its own version of the Protocols, and by 1935 the German
minister of education prescribed the work as a textbook for schools.[11]

Perhaps more than anything else, what caused the Protocols to
spread was an American edition published from May 1920 to
January 1922 in the weekly newspaper of the Ford Motor Company,
the *Dearborn Independent*. Notably, the *Independent*'s circulation
during the series increased from 72,000 to 300,000.[12] Eventually,
the articles were published in a four-volume work named after the
first of the series, *The International Jew*, which sold more than a half
million copies. A shortened version of the *Independent*'s work was
used by the Nazis as propaganda during their reign. Henry Ford
publicly apologized for the work in June 1927, but many doubted
Ford's confession was sincere because by the outbreak of World War
II *The International Jew* had been distributed in sixteen languages.[13]
The lie did not die with the cessation of World War II; in Russia the
Protocols resurged again, linked to "anti-Zionist" campaigns and
domestic and foreign policy after the Six-Day War between Israel
and the Arab nations of Egypt, Jordan, and Syria in 1967. And the
Protocols were distributed widely in Arabic, linked to a series of
holy wars and efforts to liquidate the state of Israel as early as 1948,
and with renewed intensity after the Six Days' War.[14] In 1970 the
Protocols made the best-seller list in Lebanon; in 1985 the Iranian
government published the work; in the United States it has been
sold at Nation of Islam gatherings. Identity extremists still widely
claim that perceptive readers can "confirm the genuineness" of the
Protocols.[15] Indeed, "the past hundred years have taught us that a
lie will not die out by itself."[16]

THE TURNER DIARIES

One of the most violent, hate-filled pieces of literature distributed
by racial extremists is *The Turner Diaries*, a work of fiction. The
author, using the pen name Andrew Macdonald, is William Pierce,
former Oregon State University physics professor and head of the
neo-Nazi organization National Alliance.[17] With its headquarters
located in rural Hillsboro, West Virginia, the National Alliance,

which has known chapters in at least a dozen states, was organized by Pierce in 1974. *The Turner Diaries* was first published in monthly installments in the National Alliance publication *Attack!* between 1975 and 1978. Recorded in the form of diary entries by a thirty-five-year-old, Earl Turner, and beginning in the fall of 1991, *The Turner Diaries* describes a racial war of worldwide proportions triggered by a small group of white warriors, the Organization. The first entry gives an account of the Organization's war with the Jew-controlled Federal System and the day when, eighteen months after a law was passed outlawing private ownership of firearms, the System knocked on Turner's door. After a gun was found hidden in his house, Turner was one of 800,000 arrested. He was soon released, however, and he and his unit concentrated on the Organization's goal to cleanse the United States of its alien elements and move the world into an all-white era. Turner writes: "We are truly instruments of God in the fulfillment of His Grand Design."[18]

The Bombing of a Downtown Federal Building, and the Order

In response to growing chaos wrought by Organization tactics, the System became more oppressive. For instance, the federal government designed "a computerized, universal, internal passport system."[19] Such loss of liberty could not happen without resistance, and Turner's unit was charged with blowing up the FBI headquarters housing the "passport system." They hijacked a truck, loaded it with ammonium nitrate fertilizer explosives, and delivered the bomb. After the successful detonation, Turner surveyed the destruction:

> Our worries about the relatively small size of the bomb were unfounded; the damage is immense. . . . The scene in the courtyard [of the FBI building] was one of utter devastation. . . . Approximately 700 persons were killed. . . . It is a heavy burden of responsibility for us to bear, since most of the victims of our bomb were only pawns. . . . But there is no way we can destroy the System without hurting many thousands of innocent people. . . . If we don't cut this cancer out of our living flesh—our whole race will die.[20]

Turner was up-and-coming in the Organization. And after his allegiance was tested through chemical truth serum, he was admitted into the inner sanctum of the Organization, called the Order. In the course of the war Turner was captured by the System, but because of Organization bombings, including a direct assault on the prison where Turner was held, he escaped, only to be tried on the charge of oath-breaking. Turner's sentence was merciful. He was to undertake a mission for the Order reasonably expected to result in death.

Territorial Separation and a Nuclear Threat

Not long after the judgment against Turner, the Organization stopped "wasting resources" on small-scale attacks and began targeting "power stations, fuel depots, transportation facilities, food sources, key industrial plants."[21] The goal was to hasten the decay of U.S. superstructure and create a new society based on Aryan values free from "Jewish spiritual corruption."[22] In June 1993 Turner was assigned to the Los Angeles Northwest Field Command where he would participate in an all-out assault on the System. One month later, more than sixty Organization combat cells struck simultaneously and took over the Los Angeles area and Vandenburg Air Force Base, and threatened that a military move by the System would be met with the launching of nuclear missiles targeting New York City and Tel Aviv.

Next, the program of racial deportation and extermination began. Organization troops confined blacks until they could be convoyed east into System territory; resisters were shot. What the troops found in the black neighborhoods during their roundup substantiated their views on black savagery: "[We] found gruesome evidence of one way in which the Blacks have solved their food shortage: cannibalism. They began by setting up barricades in one main street to stop cars driven by Whites. . . . The unfortunate Whites were dragged from their cars, taken into a nearby Black restaurant, butchered, cooked, and eaten."[23] As people were separated by race, a massive convoy amounting to "demographic warfare" was formed heading east. Turner described his view of one evacuation route: "As far as I could see in either direction, the unwholesome flood crept along. Not only are we getting the non-Whites out of our area, but we're . . . getting them into the enemy's area."[24]

The Day of the Rope and Nuclear War

August 1, 1993, was named the Day of the Rope because from tens of thousands of lampposts, power poles, street signs, and trees, race traitors and resisters were hung by their necks: "The politicians, the lawyers, the businessmen, the TV newscasters, the newspaper reporters and editors, the judges, the teachers, the school officials, the civic leaders, the bureaucrats, the preachers, and all the others who . . . helped promote or implement the System's racial program."[25] The hangings went on for about ten hours until Los Angeles was pacified.

The System's still massive military capabilities spurred the next phase of the revolution. A large number of nuclear warheads would be dispersed to paralyze the System's threat. For his part, Turner was to deliver four sixty-kiloton warheads to Washington, D.C. Turner concluded that "nuclear civil war" was imminent and that within a few days "the fate of the planet would be decided for all time . . . it was either the Jews or the White race."[26] In the meantime, Organization missiles from Vandenburg Air Force Base were fired at Israel and the Soviet Union, "two of world Jewry's principal nerve centers." Turner clearly stated the Organization's resolve: "We'll go to the uttermost ends of the earth to hunt down the last of Satan's spawn."[27]

Turner's Martyrdom and a White World

In the United States the Pentagon was the only hurdle to Organization victory, and the only way to penetrate the fortified Pentagon building was air delivery of a nuclear warhead. After the decision was made that Turner would be the pilot for the one-way mission, he underwent the rite of Union into the Order; at his death Turner would achieve full membership. Turner's final mission was successful, and all over the country white guerrilla fighters moved through weakened System forces. Captured white System troops were given the choice to fight for the Organization or be shot, and they were forced to prove their loyalty by bringing back "the head of a freshly killed Black or other non-White."[28] During this transitional period, tens of millions perished until on January 30, 1999, the System's generals surrendered and the Truce of Omaha was signed. Next came the "mopping-up period," when the last of the people of color were exterminated. The only remaining world power not under Organizational control by December 1999 was China. Finally, the Organization resorted to a combination of biological, chemical, and radiological weapons to wipe out the Chinese, enabling the Order to "spread its wise and benevolent rule over the earth for all time to come."[29]

THE TURNER DIARIES AND
THE OKLAHOMA CITY BOMBING

On February 11, 1992, a concerned young man wrote a letter to the *Lockport* (New York) *Union-Sun and Journal.* In it he describes the possibility of a civil war in the United States: "What is it going to take to open the eyes of our elected officials? America is in serious decline! . . . We have no proverbial tea to dump, should we instead sink a ship full of Japanese imports? Is a Civil War imminent? Do we have to shed blood to reform the current system? I hope it doesn't come to that. But it might."[30]

Three years later, on April 19, 1995, at 9:02 A.M. this same man apparently sought to light the fuse of this civil war. About five thousand pounds of fertilizer mixed with fuel oil loaded in a rental truck were detonated underneath a second-story day care facility in Oklahoma City, killing 168 people, including 19 children. Was it the work of some Mideast religious jihad bomber?[31] That was the initial fear. But a vehicle identification number on a truck axle blown two blocks from the bomb's crater led in a different direction. The issue date of the fake driver's license used by the man who rented the truck pointed to a militia and patriot rally cry: April 19, 1993, the same day the Branch Davidian's Waco enclave burned to the ground. A U.S. military veteran of the Gulf War had blown to pieces other soldiers who had survived Desert Storm.

On June 3, 1997, Timothy McVeigh was found guilty of eleven charges related to the bombing of the Alfred P. Murrah Federal Building in Oklahoma City, Oklahoma; he was sentenced to die for his crimes.[32] Later in 1997 a man McVeigh had met in the military, forty-two-year-old Terry Nichols, was convicted of conspiracy to use a weapon of mass destruction and eight counts of involuntary manslaughter.[33]

Introduced as an exhibit against McVeigh was *The Turner Diaries;* highlighted excerpts were found in an envelope in McVeigh's getaway vehicle. In an interview from prison McVeigh admitted owning and distributing the book:

> I bought the book out of [a] publication that advertised it
> as a pro-gun-rights book. That's why I bought it; that's why
> I read it. And that's why I had other people read it. In fact,
> I just recently read an interview with another Army buddy
> who said the same thing, that Tim gave me that book and
> told me to ignore the parts that looked too extreme.[34]

Table 1. *The Turner Diaries* and the Oklahoma City Bombing

Similarity	*The Turner Diaries*	Oklahoma City Bombing
Target	"FBI's national headquarters downtown"	Federal building housing FBI offices in downtown Oklahoma City
Bomb	"A little under 5,000 pounds"	Slightly less than 5,000 pounds
Explosive	"Ammonium nitrate fertilizer" and "[fuel] oil"	Ammonium nitrate fertilizer and fuel oil
Timing	9:15 A.M.	9:02 A.M.
Vehicle	"A delivery truck"	Ryder moving truck

From Richard Abanes, *Rebellion, Racism, and Religion: American Militias* (Downers Grove, Ill.: InterVarsity Press, 1996), 151–52.

The issue of gun control, which facilitates cross-pollination between the militias, Patriot groups, and Identity extremists, is evident in McVeigh's benign description of *The Turner Diaries* as a "pro-gun-rights" work. Related to this, the back of the book reads: "What will you do when they come to take your guns?" and the first entry in Turner's diary concerns the arrest of 800,000 people after the ownership of firearms was outlawed. Related to McVeigh's advice to ignore the "the parts that looked too extreme," the above summary of *The Turner Diaries* speaks for itself. Similarities between the Oklahoma City bombing and the bombing of a federal building in *The Turner Diaries* are undeniable (see table 1).

Chat on the Internet in far-right extremist circles was frequent and fiery during March 1995, one month before the bombing, as conspiracists repeatedly warned of government crackdowns.[35] On the other hand, on April 10, 1995, nine days before the bombing, a congressional report, "Militias: A Growing Danger," warned "with a sense of urgency" of possible militia activity on April 19, 1995, the second anniversary of the Waco incident.[36] McVeigh was not the first to take seriously this bible of the racist right. The influence of *The Turner Diaries* surfaced in the mid-1980s connected to a splinter group from Aryan Nations called the Order, the name also used for the secret initiates of the Organization to which the fictional Turner belonged. The Order's leader, Robert Mathews, was a National

Alliance member who tried to bring a racial war to life through a string of robberies and murder. The book also comes recommended by the Aryan Republican Army (ARA), some of whose members pleaded guilty in 1997 to a string of Midwest bank robberies.[37] In an ARA video the book is recommended for "budding young revolutionaries"; William Pierce claims to have sold nearly two hundred thousand copies over the years.[38] If the claim is to be believed, this number is remarkable considering that the book is not found in libraries or bookstores, a situation that may change since Pierce recently sold reprint rights to Lyle Stuart, Inc., a publishing house that sold more than two million copies of another controversial book, a bomb-making guide called *The Anarchist Cookbook*.[39] Pierce warns of acts of terrorism similar to the Oklahoma City bombing and suspects "a growing number of exasperated, fed-up Americans will begin engaging in terrorism on a scale that the world has never seen." The problem for Pierce is that "the Jews and the politicians and the homosexuals and the minorities and the female executives . . . have no idea how angry, how furious, normal Americans are."[40] Counterterrorism experts have highlighted the growing danger of biological and chemical weapons attacks by small fringe groups or individuals since delivery requires little technological skill, cultivation does not require expensive equipment or a great amount of space, small quantities can be lethal, and law enforcement would face difficulties tracing their origin.[41]

After the bombing, Patriots, militia members, and Identity adherents predictably cried conspiracy, claiming that the bombing was conducted by the New World Order "in order to hasten the passage of antiterrorist legislation that will literally erode our constitutional rights."[42] And there are those who accuse the federal government of using unconventional weapons against the people of the United States. Through conspiracy theories such as the "Gulf War Syndrome Cover-Up," which has nothing to do with whether U.S. soldiers were exposed to unconventional Iraqi weapons, it is asserted that Gulf War syndrome is one phase in the one-world government's plan to deplete the U.S. population.[43] From this perspective terrorist attacks by the racist right would be retaliatory.

"ON THE JEWS AND THEIR LIES"

The church reformer Martin Luther's tract "On the Jews and Their Lies" occupies a conspicuous place in racial extremist literature, despite the fact that Hitler associated Luther and the Reformation as a "Judeophile movement"[44] that weakened the German people and prepared the way for Jewry.[45] Luther's sins against the Jews cannot be taken back; such is the tragic nature of the sins of the tongue, and its closest relative, the written word. At the same time, the roots of German anti-Semitism are complex and, contrary to Luther's thinking, not concerned with the conversion of Jews or the interpretation of the Hebrew Scriptures. Yet National Socialists and Identity extremists have been able to co-opt Luther's harsh anti-Judaism for their nationalism and racial religious views.

An Inherited Blight

The virulent anti-Judaism present in Luther's later writings and the anti-Judaism and anti-Semitism evident during the Reformation were an inherited blight. There is a thread of tradition demonizing Jews from the first century into the present age. As early as the second and third centuries the Christian fathers Origen and Chrysostom warned of the Jews' black magic. With the rise to power of Constantine (306 C.E.) and the Christianizing of the Roman Empire, the church used its new power to persecute Jews. Accusations against the Jews stirred the imagination of the masses at the time of the first Crusade in 1095–99 C.E., which began and ended in the massacre of Jews.[46] The Black Death of 1348, which killed off one-half to two-thirds of Europe's population, was blamed on the Jews; between 1388 and 1519 nearly ninety expulsions were carried out within the German Empire alone.[47] Where the Jews were allowed to stay, they were subjected to heavy restrictions, economic exploitation, and persecution. On the eve of the Reformation the Jews' condition in western Europe was deplorable, and much of what we condemn as racism and anti-Semitism was a given part of the vocabulary of the sixteenth century.

A Sketch of Luther's Contemporaries

One of the most significant Roman Catholic opponents of the Reformation and a main author of the refutation of the Lutheran Augsburg Confession (written by Luther's close colleague Philip Melanchthon), Johannes Eck (1486–1543) helped shape Roman Catholic orthodoxy at the time. In Eck we have perhaps one of the most anti-Semitic authors of the time, and proof that the study of Reformation-era anti-Semitism and anti-Judaism cannot be restricted to Luther.

In response to the reformer Andreas Osiander's refutation of Jewish ritual murder, Eck accused Osiander of having been bought off by the Jewish "golden calf" and corrupted by the professor from Wittenberg, Martin Luther: "It is the devil who speaks through you Lutherans; he would like nothing better than to acquit the Jews of their murders."[48] Eck claimed to have knowledge of many "well attested" cases of Jewish ritual murder. And with the Reformation insistence on scriptural authority and the perceived overvaluation of the Hebrew Scriptures, Eck accused Lutherans of surrendering to Jewish influences.

Erasmus of Rotterdam (1466?–1536), dubbed "the prince of the humanists," believed that reform and education needed to focus on the humanizing study of the classical works of wisdom. With all of his work on toleration and education, however, Erasmus held that a reinvigorated Europe meant a Christian Europe free of Jews. He accused the Jews of staging the Peasants' War (1524–25), and he asserted that even a baptized Jew was not a full-fledged Christian. In addition, in contrast to the reformers' perceived overvaluation of the Hebrew Scriptures, Erasmus was cautious of Judaic influences. Erasmus coined the now famous statement, "If to hate Jews is the proof of genuine Christians, then we are all excellent Christians." He was an advocate for tolerance and intellectual freedom, but his tolerance did not reach as far as the "most pernicious plague and bitterest foe of the teachings of Jesus Christ," Judaism.[49]

Amidst the common and virulent anti-Semitism, in 1529 a tract refuting accusations of Jewish ritual murder appeared, "Whether It Be True and Credible That the Jews Secretly Strangulate Christian Children and Make Use of Their Blood," known now to be the work of Andreas Osiander (1498–1552). Osiander was appointed in 1520 as a Hebrew instructor to the Augustinian monastery in Nuremberg and was actively involved with the followers of Luther. Osiander, an exception in his milieu, confronted accusations with information. He pointed out that Moses prohibited both murder and the ritual use of blood, that Christians in the early church were also accused of ritual murder, and that in the tried cases in his day the guilty parties had turned out to be Christians. Osiander warned that those who accuse the Jews of murder should be suspect, especially those who might gain from such scapegoating because of financial debt or lethal child abuse.

Justas Jonas (1493–1555) was also Luther's colleague and later best man at Luther's wedding. Although Jonas supported Luther's cause on most points, he sided with Osiander when it came to the

Jewish question. Following the apostle Paul in Romans, Jonas claimed that Christians are guests in the family of Abraham and grafted into Israel (Rom. 11:17). Jonas asserted that with the coming of Jesus Christ, the old and new covenants had come together by the will of a God not fazed by the disobedience of Jews or Christians. While still emphasizing mission to the Jews and hoping for their conversion, Jonas was primarily concerned with the conversion of the heathen. He called for the church and Luther to see in the Jews companions in destiny and to pray for them, "seeing that even among us, not all that purports to be Christian . . . deserves the name."[50]

Luther's Mixed Legacy

Generally speaking, Luther seems to fall somewhere between the polemics of Eck and Erasmus, on the one side, and the more forbearing stance of Osiander and Jonas, on the other. If Luther was at any time a friend and defender of the Jews, he was these in sharp contrast to the prevailing sentiments; if an enemy, he carried on the legacy of the Middle Ages.[51] And while Eck and others were pursuing the Jewish child murderers, for Luther the issue was the interpretation of the Holy Scriptures and theological truth and error. Suppression of this theological foundation has resulted in highly unbalanced presentations. There is no independent theme on the Jews in Luther's theology and no collective disdain for a race of born murderers or liars. Luther saw the baptized Jew, Turk, German, and Gentile as unqualifiedly the people of God.

"That Jesus Christ Was Born a Jew"

The 1523 work titled "That Jesus Christ Was Born a Jew" was Luther's response to Eck's public charges that Luther believed "Jesus was conceived of the seed of Joseph, and that Mary was not a virgin."[52] Luther's work was greeted with joy by many Jews, although his reading of the Hebrew Scriptures as all pointing to the Christ (a christological reading) should have given pause. Citations from the work illustrate its tone and also Luther's characteristic polemics:

> The popes, bishops, sophists, and monks—the crude asses' heads—have hitherto so treated the Jews that anyone who wished to be a good Christian would almost have had to become a Jew. If I had been a Jew and had seen such dolts

and blockheads govern and teach the Christian faith, I would sooner have become a hog than a Christian.[53]

They have dealt with the Jews as if they were dogs rather than human beings; they have done little else than deride them and seize their property, when they baptize them they show them nothing of Christian doctrine or life, but only subject them to popishness and monkery. . . . If the apostles, who also were Jews, had dealt with us Gentiles as we Gentiles deal with the Jews, there would have never been a Christian among the Gentiles.[54]

The late Rabbi Marc Tanenbaum, commenting on the inheritance Luther received from his medieval predecessors, observed that it was "remarkable" that Luther "could have passed through a period of philo-Semitic sympathy for Jews."[55] But Luther it seems, toward the end of his life, suffered a "theological failure of nerve."[56] Trying with his life to communicate the gospel, when faced with the unbelief of committed Jews, he no longer let God be God, and he consigned the Jews to God's wrath. But the Jews were not the only ones left out as Luther continued to set boundaries to protect the church. The modern view of a pluralistic society in which people with different faiths could live together was not part of Luther's worldview.

The Same Man? "On the Jews and Their Lies"

Toward the end of his life, Luther wrote "On the Jews and Their Lies" (1545). The lengthiest section of the work is dedicated to his argument for a christological interpretation of the Hebrew Scriptures. Luther's recommendations to the authorities on how to deal with the Jews are most often cited by racial extremists. Although "That Jesus Christ Was Born a Jew" far outsold "On the Jews and Their Lies" in Luther's day, citations from the later work reveal its allure for racial extremists:

I shall give you my sincere advice: First, to set fire to their synagogues or schools and to bury and cover with dirt whatever will not burn, so that no man will ever again see stone or cinder of them. This is to be done in honor of our Lord and of Christendom.[57]

Such a desperate, thoroughly evil, poisonous, and devilish lot are these Jews, who for these fourteen hundred years have been and still are our plague, our pestilence, and our misfortune.[58]

There is no limit to the use of such violent words. Although recognizing the complexity of the man and the issue, Rabbi Tanenbaum perceptively pointed out that what was unique about Luther's targeting of the Jews was their relative helplessness; they were at the mercy of their Catholic and Protestant rulers.[59]

Explanation Is Not Excuse

Once the gospel of God's justification of the ungodly had been rediscovered as the foundation for the church, Luther perceived the devil's assaults as increasing in intensity. These circumstances, for Luther, thrust the church into a battle for truth against the Romans, heretics, Turks, Jews, and obstinate Christians—in Luther's words, "we miserable Christians ourselves." Luther believed that the last phase of history had dawned and that proclamation centered on God's justification of the ungodly was the last chance for Jews and Christians alike. No pope, no inquisitions, no government reforms could save humankind; a Jew-free Germany would not bring in the kingdom of God. Salvation was found only in God's grace. But Luther was at times virulently anti-Judaic and clearly broke God's commandments protecting human beings and demanding love of one's neighbor. How can one account for these disparate messages of the reformer? Various factors are cited, with truth to be found in a combination.[60] Though not offered as excuses, the following aspects offer insight into Luther's later anti-Judaism:

- *The health factor.* In 1536, Luther suffered severely from kidney stones that blocked his ureters until February 1537. He barely survived. The result of the blockage was a high level of uremic poisoning known to cause personality changes. Luther was always highly polemical, but in the years following his uremic poisoning he wrote some of his crudest essays. Luther's virulent writings against the Jews are consistent with his handling of almost everyone with whom he disagreed, especially in the 1540s. In December 1544 Luther experienced severe angina, and in February 1546 a heart attack killed him. This evaluation directly contradicts the racial extremists' assertion that Luther wrote "On the Jews and Their Lies" in "the prime of life."[61]

- *The proselytizing factor.* In a letter written declining help to the Jewish leader Josel of Rosheim in 1537, Luther recounts a visit paid to him in 1536 by three Jews with whom he debated the interpretation of the Hebrew Scriptures. During the visit Luther became frustrated and vowed not to dialogue again with the Jews.[62] Because he perceived the church to be under siege and approaching the end times, Luther's concerns were magnified. By the 1540s the time of proselytizing had passed, and Luther wrote not for the unconverted, but for partisan ears in order to defend against the Catholics, the Turks, the Christian fanatics, and Jewish exegesis and proselytizing.
- *The apocalyptic factor.* Driven by biblical expectation, the Reformation, and apocalyptic rumors, Luther lived in anticipation of Christ's imminent return. And in "the later 1530 and 1540s, this expectation boiled over" against the Jews. The last days allowed for no compromise with forces perceived to be at odds with the cause of the gospel.[63] Over against Judaism, the battle over the true interpretation of the Hebrew Scriptures represented a staking out of a claim for Jesus Christ in the world during the last days.[64]

In recent years heartening dialogue and action have occurred within major Lutheran Church bodies and between Lutherans and Jews. For example, the Lutheran World Federation's Fourth Consultation on the Church and the Jewish People called for the removal from among Christians "of any hatred of the Jews and any sort of teaching of contempt for Judaism," and confessed that in his later years Luther "made certain vitriolic statements about the Jews that Lutheran Churches today universally reject."[65] It is always the church's calling to confess the sin in its midst that prevents the proclamation of the gospel, separate out the essential teachings of the faith that witness to the truth of the Word of God, and renounce teachings of both the past and the present that are not appropriate or relevant to the Christian witness.

6

USING POLITICAL
ISSUES AS A COVER

We are having difficulty sustaining dialogue at this time,
having trouble communicating in a meaningful way.

—On the Montana Freemen's standoff,
April 1996[1]

dentity extremists gather with various groups and communities
putting forth and supporting seemingly benign or disparate
agendas. These more accessible agendas operate as a cover
concealing from the public their racial faith. What we hear of and
see are noisy tax protesters, "patriots" concerned about the corrupt
federal government, citizens deeply concerned about the right to
bear arms, or protests concerning the government's handling of
Waco and Ruby Ridge.[2] Though their actions were rooted in their
racist Identity faith, countless times the Freemen were vaguely and
shallowly described as an "anti-government group whose followers
do not recognize the authority of the federal government,"[3] or a
group who "refuse to pay taxes and question the validity of U.S.
currency."[4]

BRIDGE ISSUES AS COVERS FOR RACISM

A popular reaction toward the various agendas promoted by
Identity adherents is that their causes are worthy and their courage
admirable, but they are attempting to bring about change in mis-
guided ways. However, these bridge issues, which connect with

Table 2. Bridge Issues and Identity Sources

Bridge Issues	Identity Sources
Taxes Tax protesting Tax evasion	• "No direct taxes on the People of Israel!!"[a] • "God gave us the new land of Zion. . . . Why are you allowing [public servants] to tax His Land that He gave us."[b] • "About 20% of all Americans, having never taken the 'Socialist Security card,' or paid any federal taxes, are the last true citizens . . . the lawful people of the Republic."[c]
Stockpiling weapons Gun control Militias Survivalism	• "This is a religious war."[d] • "Satan's kids must go!"[e] • "This IS a battle, 'The Children of Light vs. The Children of Darkness.' Yes, a Racial Holy War."[f] • "[Jesus'] intended purpose is that His racial kinsmen are to have dominion over this earth."[g]
Government corruption New World Order Conspiracy theories Local autonomy	• "Washington, D.C. is the seat of . . . Satan."[h] • "The one-world conspiracy facing us in our day is a culmination of the mischief wrought by Cain and his descendants."[i] • "The Seed of the Serpent sit in high places as the movers and shakers of history."[j]
Citizenship Constitutional rights Patriotism Immigration	• "We declare our God-given right as descendants and members of the seedline who founded these United States to continue our racial existence."[k] • "Do not settle and raise your children in an area with high serpent population."[l] • "[The] Constitution . . . insured freeman status to all male Anglo-Saxon Israelites and their families."[m]
Laws Courts Judges Juries	• "[These] do not apply to the People of the Posterity, i.e., white race/American Nationals."[n] • "[The] enemies of Christ have taken their Jewish Communist Manifesto, and incorporated it into the Statutory Law of our country, and threw our Constitution and our Christian Common Law . . . into the garbage can."[o] • "We are not to allow women nor foreigners (colored people, jews, and/or citizens of the United States) to rule over us. . . . We must appoint our own Men of Israel."[p]
Almighty God Jesus Christ Christian	• "Remember that the Bible was written for only one race of people."[q] • "Our Race, the White Race, is God's chosen Race."[r] • "The Seed of the Serpent cannot be saved."[s]

[a]$100 Billion Freemen Lien, 3. [b]*Freeman Edict,* 11. [c]Nord Davis Jr., *Sui Juris* (Topton, N.C.: Northpoint Teams, 1994), 13. [d]$100 Billion Freemen Lien, 16. [e]Mohr, *Satan's Kids,* 34. [f]Posse Comitatus Internet edition at <www.webexpert.net/posse/p2.html>. [g]*Yesterday: The Tribes of Israel. Today: The White Christian Nations.* [h]$100 Billion Freemen Lien, 12. [i]Mohr, *The Birthright,* 10. [j]Gayman, *Two Seeds,* 26. [k]Barkun, *Religion and the Racist Right,* 231. [l]Gayman, *Two Seeds,* 297. [m]Gayman, *The Duties of a Christian Citizen,* 142. [n]$100 Billion Freemen Lien, 10. [o]Statement by Gordon Kahl, 1983 (4 pp.). [p]*Freeman Edict,* 19. [q]Ibid., 3. [r]Emry, *Paul and Joseph,* 35. [s]Gayman, *Two Seeds,* 9.

broad societal discontent, are public expressions of a private faith. What is at stake is not whether their methods of protest or efforts for social change are too crude, but is the spread of a comprehensive racial theology. Table 2 lists controversial mainstream issues important to a wide range of people, which are also bridge issues with roots in the Identity worldview.

The use of bridge issues with broad appeal allows racial extremists to have "one foot in the political mainstream and the other in the fringe."[5] In terms of the pool of citizens with whom one might be able to connect, Identity's bridging makes sense. After all, how many people want to pay more taxes? Who really thinks that all public servants are out to serve the public and not their own self-interests? When the new racial extremists talk about these bridge issues, people listen. But these bridge issues are just the tip of the iceberg, as the following examples illustrate.

NO TAXES ON WHITE ISRAEL

Many Identity disciples protest the federal tax system. But these are no mere disgruntled citizens who believe tax money is being used for morally objectionable purposes. When the issue of taxes is exposed as an Identity bridge issue, it becomes clear that what drives the tax issue is a comprehensive racial theology. Identity adherents believe that the United States is the literal promised land given to the white race; this belief pervades material such as *America: Zion of God* and *The United States in Prophecy*.[6] Consequently, white Israel cannot be taxed for the land that God has given them. In addition, Identity extremists believe they are obeying the directive of their racial kinsman Jesus.

> Passing ordinances pursuant to the Word of Almighty God would eliminate all direct taxes on the People of the Posterity; for did not Jesus, Emmanuel, say this about taxes on Israel. "What do you think, Simon? From whom do the kings of the earth take toll or tribute? From their sons or others?" And when he said, "From others," Jesus said to him, "Then the sons are free." (Matt. 17:25–26; KJV)[7]

For Identity, the "others" mentioned by Jesus are aliens residing in white Israel's United States, such as Jews, people of color, or anyone who has signed a contract with the satanic government in the form of a social security card, marriage license, or tax form; these "others" may legally be taxed. The "sons" to whom Jesus alludes are white Israelite males; Jesus authoritatively and for all time declares they are free from paying taxes. In the Identity world, taxes become an ultimate issue related to faith in a racial god, and people are willing to die before they submit to Satan. That was certainly the case for Gordon Kahl, a decorated World War II veteran who grew up on the farm his father homesteaded in North Dakota. Kahl inaugurated his battle with the satanic government in 1967 by refusing to pay taxes, notifying the Internal Revenue Service that he would no longer "pay tithes to the Synagogue of Satan."[8] Acting on the presumption that the Jew-controlled government's control of farmers was preliminary to the control of all people in the United States, Kahl joined the growing Posse Comitatus movement in 1973. A statement written by Kahl reveals the Identity roots of his tax protesting:

> We are a conquered and occupied nation; conquered and occupied by the Jews, and their hundreds or maybe thousands of front organizations doing their un-Godly work. They have two objectives in their goal of ruling the world. Destroy Christianity and the White race. We are engaged in a struggle to the death between the people of the Kingdom of God, and the Kingdom of Satan.[9]

When he was pulled over north of Medina, North Dakota, by federal marshals and began a shoot-out, Kahl had just left a meeting concerning how he and others could implement the proceedings of the Third Continental Congress to restore the power of the U.S. Constitution and put their nation back under "Christian Common Law." Kahl was eventually killed in Arkansas by the FBI a month after the Medina shoot-out.

Still today, the ultimacy of an important Identity bridge issue, taxes, results in the paranoid claim that a tax protester was so important to the satanic government that those killed in the shoot-out had abandoned everything in the attempt to murder a "patriot" on a public highway. In the Identity world a man who viewed the income tax as a tithe to the "Synagogue of Satan," which gave him the religious justification to kill, whose protests resulted in the deaths of four men and the incarceration of two others (including his son, Yorie) for the rest of their lives, and in the wake of whose actions countless families were deeply wounded, is still touted as a hero and an inspiration for today's white warriors.

Two more examples of Identity bridge issues are veiled behind concern for the legitimacy of juries, and religious and scholarly labels used by racial communities and organizations. When the Montana Freemen were "negotiating" with federal law enforcement officers for the end of the standoff in Jordan, Montana, one of the Freemen's prerequisites for surrender was that a "lawful jury of peers" be assembled for their trial. The Freemen argued that if they were brought to trial, the federal government would "never be able to find a lawful jury of peers," but would "only be able to select a jury of foreigners."[10] And not long before these events, it was matter-of-factly reported in a newspaper that William Stanton, convicted of criminal syndicalism (the advocacy of crime to accomplish political ends) for involvement in the Freemen's attempt to set up their own court in Garfield County, Montana, claimed during his court proceedings that there were "no freemen" at his trial to sit on his jury.[11] What was either neglected or not known was the centrality of this bridge issue to the Identity worldview. For Identity, a "lawful jury of peers" would never include women, Jews, people of color, or whites who have signed a contract with the current unlawful government. In Identity, "peers" means exclusively white "Christian" males who have "expatriated" from the satanic government: "We are not to allow women nor foreigners (colored people, jews, and/or citizens of the United States) to rule over us. . . . We must appoint our own Men of Israel."[12]

Examples of bridging with the use of seemingly benign or even inspiring language are found in the names of racial communities and organizations. Identity churches proclaiming that the white race is Israel and Jews are descendants of Satan, such as the Church of Jesus Christ, Christian in Hayden Lake, Idaho, or the Church of Israel in Schell City, Missouri, cannot be exposed by their names. Neither can one readily identify Identity's "colleges" teaching the racial faith, such as the American Institute of Theology in Harrison, Arkansas, because of the same deceptive veneers. And despite the harmless-sounding names, the publications from which Identity believers coast to coast get their news on the progress of ZOG and statistics and rhetoric denying the Holocaust are the *Jubilee Newspaper* in Midpines, California, and the *Journal of Historical Review* in Newport Beach, California, respectively. The Christian Patriot Association (CPA), a "Christian Political Education Association," sounds innocent enough. However, the largest section of CPA's catalog is dedicated to "Christianity-Race-Religion" and includes a large selection of the most popular racial extremist literature including *Death Penalty for Race-Mixers* and *The Satanic Seedline*.[13] Given this survey of Identity bridge issues, we now explore how these issues are expressed in and through the military, political, and social agendas born out of the racial worldview.

THE MILITARY AGENDA:
A WAR AGAINST A SPREADING EVIL

A statement from *Censored Bible Teachings* summarizes this bridge issue: "God requires gun ownership."[14] In racial extremist literature the rhetoric resounds; the satanic federal government has turned against its citizens. Warnings go out that people are in danger of losing their right to bear arms and the ability to protect themselves against government tyranny. But the objectives of the Montana Freemen and other loosely connected groups are much broader and deeper than generally covered. Taking gun control as an example, and using the biblical images that shape the Identity worldview, if you are fighting Satan's kids here on earth and are fighting for the survival of God's eternal plans, you had better have big enough weapons to engage the enemy. In light of this perception the recent resurgence in activity of racial extremism has logically paralleled the resurgence in groups calling themselves militias.

For Identity adherents and their allies, Waco and Ruby Ridge are about all-American people exercising their constitutional right to bear arms who were slaughtered or arrested by a government whose goal is to disarm all patriotic Americans; for them, "in both cases the government shot people who only wanted to own guns and enjoy their own religion."[15] Although it was discovered that the Branch Davidians had more than forty illegal machine guns on their compound, any government regulation of firearms is perceived as unqualifiedly oppressive; Identity pastor Pete Peters compares those who are for any kind of gun control to the mass murderers Lenin, Stalin, and Mao Tse-Tung.[16]

Militia leaders are using guns as a symbol for freedom and liberty, and stepping over the very blurred boundary into the Identity worldview, white warriors need to defend against Satan's kids. Those who regulate guns, they claim, work for the satanic New World Order, which is confiscating guns first; next will follow the ban of free speech, free practice of religion, and every other freedom. In one conspiratorial scenario, as soon as Patriots are disarmed, the UN can effectively invade, set up a new government, and detain Patriots in concentration camps. Identity adherents and their militia and

Patriot counterparts are claiming that they need to be able to defend themselves against the satanic government and must not be "outgunned"; one can only assume they believe that since the United States government has nuclear weapons, they must have them as well. David Darby of the Clark County Militia substantiates this illogic: "It doesn't matter if it's a pistol, a rifle, an assault rifle, a tank or a battleship if you could afford it."[17] That guns are perceived as a legitimate check on power in the United States has been called the insurrectionist theory of the Second Amendment:[18]

> What militia leaders are relying upon in their "insurrectionist theory" is not the Second Amendment as much as the generalized principle, expressed by Mao and many others, that power comes from the barrel of a gun. . . . The right to have arms in order to threaten government necessarily implies a right to use them for that purpose. (Otherwise, how could it be a valid check on power?) The Constitution set out many ways to reform government, even to remake it entirely. Elections. Petition. The free press. Impeachment. Constitutional amendments. No government provides for the right of groups of armed, disgruntled citizens to revolt by blowing up and gunning down government officials. That is called sedition, assassination, and treason, and is punishable by law.[19]

The term "well-regulated militia" is also twisted to meet the needs of the self-styled militias, including the racial variety. The amendment's intent was never to create private militias. Rather, the intent was that the militia would be well regulated by the government. The United States Constitution, in article 1, section 8, clause 15, gives Congress the power "to provide for calling forth the Militia to execute the Laws of the Union, suppress Insurrections and repel Invasions." And clause 16 gives Congress the power "to provide for organizing, arming, and disciplining the Militia" and employing them where and when needed, and reserves for the states the training and "the Appointment of the Officers." The highest courts of the land have held that the modern embodiment of the well-regulated militia is the National Guard, which does not use privately owned guns. But militias and Patriot groups claim the National Guard has been "federalized," making it invalid and creating a militia vacuum that they perceive as their duty to fill. Obviously, the gun remains a volatile issue in our culture and in politics, an issue

that needs to be addressed without the influence of distorted interpretations of the Constitution, which have led to the delusional
conclusion that "shooting American public officials is a patriotic
duty."[20] Samuel Sherwood, the former head of the United States
Militia Association, Idaho's main militia, has framed the issue this
way: "Go up and look legislators in the face because some day you
may be forced to blow it off."[21]

Racial extremist violence at times seems to erupt randomly
and unexpectedly. For one savage example, in February 1999 John
William King was given the death penalty by a Jasper, Texas, jury for
chaining forty-nine-year-old James Byrd Jr., a black man, to the back
of a pickup truck and dragging him three miles until he was dead.
Writings by King seized from his apartment cast him as a hero fighting in a race war.[22]

But Identity's more intentional military agenda takes different
forms. Louis Beam, who recently moved to Idaho from Texas,
where he ran a white separatist paramilitary outfit called the Texas
Emergency Reserve and was Grand Dragon of the Knights of the Ku
Klux Klan, has rejuvenated the concept of Leaderless Resistance.
He asserts that the survivable racist organization will be small,
loosely knit "cell systems" so that the battle "presents no single
opportunity for the Federals to destroy a significant portion of
the resistance."[23] His intentions are clear in a quote from a Klan
newsletter: "Our Order intends to take part in the Physical and
Spiritual Racial Purification of ALL those countries which have
been traditionally considered White Lands in Modern Times . . . IN
SUMMARY: This continent will be white or it will not be at all."[24]
The Aryan Republican Army (ARA) has been serving its racial god
and funding the war chest with a string of bank robberies in the
Midwest. Four members of the ARA, known as "the Midwestern
Bank Bandits," are suspected of committing at least eighteen bank
robberies in Iowa, Kansas, Kentucky, Missouri, Nebraska, Ohio, and
Wisconsin between 1992 and 1995. Three members pleaded guilty
in 1997 and await their trials. One of the men can be seen in a two-
hour recruitment video for the ARA holding up a copy of the book
The Vigilantes of Christendom, which advocates guerrilla holy war
conducted by individual white warriors, and urging viewers to read
it carefully as "a handbook for the revolution."[25] White warriors—
including members of the New Order led by an ex-Klan leader
and caught planning a campaign of domestic terrorism including
assassinations, bombings, robberies, and poisoning of city water
supplies, and indicted in 1998 for conspiracy to receive and possess

machine guns and destructive devices—are building on those who have gone before them, such as the group the Order. The Order declared war on the United States government beginning in the early 1980s.[26]

Known by its members as the Bruders Schweigen, or Silent Brotherhood, the Order was founded by Robert Mathews in northeast Washington State in 1983 when he brought together a small group committed to overthrowing the Zionist Occupation Government and establishing a northwest "White American Bastion." Bruce Carroll Pierce stated the group's goals in Identity terms: "We declare our God-given right as descendants and members of the seed-line who founded these United States to continue our racial existence . . . so that our people may fulfill the mission allotted them by the Creator of the universe."[27] Toward this goal, they engaged in counterfeiting, armed robbery, and murder. In July 1984, members robbed a Brink's armored car in northern California and made off with $3.8 million. Mathews is reported to have distributed the money among racial extremist organizations including National Alliance, the Ku Klux Klan, White Aryan Resistance, Aryan Nations, and Church of Israel. The most publicized criminal act by the Order was the 1984 murder of Alan Berg, a Jewish radio talk-show host from Denver who often debated extremists on his program. After the murder, Mathews was eventually tracked down in Whidbey Island, Washington, where in December 1984 he was killed in a shoot-out with federal authorities. Before he was killed, Mathews communicated his terms of surrender: "parts of eastern Washington, Idaho, and Montana set aside as an Aryan homeland."[28] Members of the Order still incarcerated at this writing consider themselves POWs, and the Order's Declaration of War is still circulating on the Internet:

> We hereby declare ourselves to be a free and sovereign people. We claim a territorial imperative which will consist of the entire North American continent north of Mexico. . . . Let friend and foe alike be made aware. This is war! . . . Therefore, for Blood, Soil, Honor, and for the future of our children, we commit ourselves to Battle. Amen.[29]

While the military agenda of some Identity groups and their allies is quite obvious, for others it is not and therefore cannot be taken as the sole determiner when exposing Identity. In an article published in the Identity newspaper, the *Jubilee Newspaper*, reporter Jeff

Randall reflects on current racial extremist trends: "The political playing field is becoming the new battle ground and the new camo uniform is a three-piece suit. Many militia members and sympathizers are running for office."[30]

Related to claims that there might be a "toned down" form of Identity, I received a personal letter from the pastor of the Church of Israel located in Schell City, Missouri, who was concerned that all Identity groups might be associated with vigilante tendencies. He objected to being stereotyped as a "white supremacist" because he did not advocate armed rebellion, and he preferred to categorize himself as one who would "fall into the religious right." Cited as proof of his more "moderate" position, in the book sent along with the letter, *The Duties of a Christian Citizen: A Handbook on Christian Citizenship*, this Identity pastor instructs followers to pay their taxes and live peacefully with the government and claims that the only thing that distances them from mainstream Christianity is that they teach that the Anglo-Saxon people of the earth are the genetic descendants of the biblical Israel.[31] But this Identity pastor holds in common with his Identity kinsmen the beliefs that Satan has literal children in the form of Jews, people of color are inferior beasts, and the Bible was written for the white race exclusively.

Variations in the expressions of the military agenda, and in some cases the lack of any such agenda, teaches that focusing on the military agenda reveals tendencies and trends of Identity groups but does not get to the heart of the issue. The Church of Israel seems to be less violent in its ways. But undergirding the Order, the Freemen, Aryan Nations, *and* the Church of Israel is the violently dehumanizing Identity doctrine. Despite these military variances, it must be stated in uncompromising terms: whether it includes guns or not, the theology of Identity is grossly perverted and does violence to both the basic humanity we all share and the Jewish and Christian witness to the world.

THE POLITICAL AGENDA: RACIAL NATIONALISM AND EXTREME LOCALISM

Identity's political agendas are expressed in various ways. Among the legal avenues pursued by racial extremists in the political sphere are attempts to radically reform the existing U.S. legal system to bring it into agreement with racial interpretations of the laws in the Bible, and support for political candidates who advance Identity agendas.[32] Identity attempts to revamp the U.S. legal system differ from the attempts of some Christians to bring biblical law to bear on public life. Identity believers are acting on the conviction that the white race is biblical Israel residing in the literal promised land, and "Church and State represent the undivided government of God."[33] Therefore, any imperatives made to Israel are perceived as directed to "God's Kingdom people," white Christians, and must be instituted at all levels of life. Also troubling are the public officials who pander to and help legitimize the militias, Patriot groups, Identity organizations, and conspiracy theorists by seeing in them only political allies. Public officials who see only votes coming from racial extremists must address the violent rhetoric, anti-Semitism, paranoid conspiracy theories, and racism that drive such groups and must take responsibility for rhetoric that vilifies other human beings.

More problematic political expressions of Identity faith include the creation of survivalist communities that avoid contact with the larger society and reject the legitimacy of the present government, and the formation of parallel local political groups claiming that their "governments" are the only legitimate ones. Such isolationist tendencies have the potential to lead to confrontation with the larger society. Inevitably, the larger society will make some kind of claim on those who reject the government and attempt to segregate themselves. A 1982 incident in northern Idaho involving attempts to form Nehemiah Township and the Montana Freemen's more recent attempt to establish Justus Township are just two examples of this political expression. In Idaho in 1982 a who's who of racial extremists including Aryan Nations leader Richard Butler and Klan Imperial Wizard Thom Robb filed the "Nehemiah Township Charter and Common Law Contract" in Kootenia County, perceiving that the action made their claims to jurisdiction valid over a state of "Aryan Freemen" governed by "Anglo-Saxon law." Within their township, the posse would be responsible for law enforcement while a militia would be dispatched, where needed, outside township boundaries. The Freemen of Montana, upon establishing their Justus Township, "a free sovereign and independent State," created their own "one Supreme Court." For them too, the posse was to enforce the "Law of the Land." And anyone who would obstruct their "Justice" was subject to immediate arrest. Identity political agendas that are unambiguously illegal include attempting to overthrow the current government through terrorism and guerrilla warfare and conspiring toward territorial succession in order to create a separate "white Christian" nation.[34]

Paper Wars

The racial war is being fought not only with guns, bombs, poison, and claims to land. Paper wars waged against the satanic government have spread across the nation. An IRS investigator testified in the Freemen case that approximately 3,400 Freemen checks totaling $15.5 billion were written on a closed Norwest Bank account between 1994 and 1996. For example, a California woman who was a disciple of Leroy Schweitzer of the Montana Freemen was convicted of fraud and money laundering in Los Angeles in October 1996 for issuing some eight thousand bogus government checks, many of which were signed by Schweitzer and which netted her an estimated $1 million.[35] And two men were found guilty of fraud charges in the San Jose, California, District Court in July 1997 stemming from writing bogus "Certified Bankers Checks" and "Comptroller Warrants" sent to banks, mortgage companies, credit card companies, and the IRS. The checks were often written exceeding the amount owed, and a refund of overpayment was requested. The total value of the worthless checks used for the conviction exceeded $12 million. Both men had attended seminars in the fall of 1995 at the Montana Freemen compound south of Roundup.[36] For some, the fraudulent papers used to pay off mortgages, land payments, equipment, and other bills may be a way out of perceived desperate times calling for desperate measures. But for those looking through the lens of Identity theology, the fraudulent liens, checks, and money orders are paper terrorism conducted against Satan and the powers of darkness in order to destroy the existing demonic economic infrastructure.

The wordy papers used in the race war are not just lawsuits or liens, but also include declarations of sorts. The Declaration of Citizenship by a Montana Freeman who made the national news during the Jordan standoff in 1996 included facts deemed essential for full citizenship. Notably, John Trochmann, leader of the Militia of Montana, who continuously denies his connections with the racist right, filed an almost identical document at the Sanders County courthouse in January 1992: "I am a White Male"; "Both my parents . . . were of the White Race"; "My Mother's parents were of the White Race"; "My Father's parents were of the White Race"; "I am not a federal 'citizen of the United States' under the so-called 14th Amendment." Also, during their time at Justus Township, the Freemen posted "Wanted" posters on numerous public officials including the chief U.S. district judge; the posters displayed a photograph of the judge and offered $1 million "dead or alive."[37]

Government workers and law enforcement officers are not the only persons targeted. The confiscation of property for nonpayment of taxes is looked upon as an "act of war" against "the Kingdom of Heaven and the Kingdom of God."[38] When a Montana Freeman's pickup truck was confiscated, a high school student who purchased the auctioned vehicle was threatened and sued for $5 million; Dave's Towing-Exxon was sued for the same amount for towing the vehicle away.[39] And I, a public minister, was targeted after speaking at an education event held in Jordan during the Freemen's standoff called "The Confessing Church Meets the Extremists of the 90's." Soon after the event I was charged with perjury, slander, conspiracy, treason, and inciting a riot, and I was sued for $100 billion.

Identity's paper wars are costing U.S. taxpayers millions of dollars. In 1995 the head of the Montana attorney general's local government assistance bureau estimated that he spent one-quarter of his time dealing with Freemen and militia cases: "There's no other single area that I have spent so much time on this year." According to the chief of the Montana Justice Department's Legal Services Bureau, in 1995 common-law actions against the government made up thirty of the agency's forty open cases.[40] The situation is even more serious at the county level, where county sheriffs' departments weigh bills for housing prisoners, additional security, unbudgeted equipment, and employee hours.[41]

Racial Electoral Politics

The strategy for racial extremists to "go mainstream" politically is done in tension with the danger of legitimizing the existing system. And there are those who think the effort is pointless because there is "no hope to out-vote the alien power that rules" the Aryan people.[42] Some Identity figures have paved the way for the current trend of binding racial agendas to more mainstream politics. James Wickstrom, who was a Posse Comitatus leader in Wisconsin and a caustic Identity leader, ran for the U.S. Senate in 1980 and captured 16,000 votes. He lost handily, but the number of votes he garnered seems astonishing given his toxic Identity beliefs: "These fools [the federal government] think we are a political organization, not realizing that we have declared a Holy War against them."[43] In the mid-1970s Tom Metzger entered the Identity ministry and joined the Ku Klux Klan. In 1979 Metzger founded a group that mutated into his most recent organization, the paramilitary-oriented White Aryan Resistance (WAR), and ran for the San Diego county supervisor position, gaining 11,000 votes. In 1980 he won the Democratic nomination for Congress with 43,000 votes but lost in the general election. And in 1982, Metzger ran for the U.S. Senate and managed to gain 7.8 percent of the vote, 75,593 votes, and these with his racial extremism by no means a secret.[44] Metzger had found what followers are exploiting: "You don't make change having fiery crosses out in cow pastures. You make change by invading the halls of Congress and the Statehouse."[45]

No other racial extremist has had success at the polls equal to that of the one-time Republican state representative for Jefferson Parish, Louisiana, David Duke. Despite Duke's racial ideology and Identity connections that left "a paper trail that was twenty years long,"[46] he was elected to serve in the Louisiana House of Representatives in February 1989. Hiding behind the banner of "equal rights for all, special rights for none,"[47] Duke exploited a zone of friction and was able to gain the ears of racial extremists, those who flirt with racial extremism, and those attracted to the more mainstream controversial issues such as affirmative action and government corruption. Evidence of Duke's widespread appeal is revealed in that only 18 percent of his campaign funds for the 1989 Senate race were from Louisiana; donations came from all fifty states.[48] After Duke's election his ties to racial extremism continued, and he sold racial extremist literature from his campaign office. As late as the summer of 1989 people could purchase through him the fictional account of a racial world war, *The Turner Diaries*; a work that denies the Holocaust, *The Myth of the Six Million*; and Hitler's manifesto, *Mein Kampf* (My Struggle).[49]

Duke's plans are far more ambitious than serving Louisiana as state representative. In an article originally published in 1984 in the *National Association for the Advancement of White People News*, he proposed geographic relocation for "unassimilable minorities" into areas such as Hawaii, southern California, and Florida. The Louisiana Republican Party newsletter distributed after the elections in 1989 described Duke innocently as one who "ran on a conservative platform."[50] For his part Duke effectively expressed his racial worldview through a vocabulary purged of classic racial language and effectively used the media and bridge issues to gain a hearing. Many with Identity connections have dropped the swastika and goose stepping and have donned three-piece suits, entered the mainstream political realm, and clothed their Identity worldview in rhetoric of equality and democracy. But after all, taking the Militia of Montana as an example, despite the Trochmanns' mainstream rhetoric, they have not attempted to influence the ballot box, but are distributing literature and tapes on how to conduct war.

THE SOCIAL AGENDA: WHITE NEIGHBORS

One of the most urgent Identity agendas is advancing a racial "preservationist ethic,"[51] which results in the drive to be racially separatist: "From Genesis to Revelation the Word of God warns us to not mix the races."[52] According to Identity's interpretation of biblical law, "race-mixing is an abomination in the sight of Almighty God," the Christian is "duty-bound to practice racial segregation in all areas of family life" since "God and the Bible demand segregation and the separation of the races," and segregation is "practiced by God himself."[53] It stands to reason that if you believe Satan has offspring here on earth, they are to be avoided: "Do not settle and raise your children in an area with high Serpent population. . . . Beware of going to any physician who is of the Serpent Seed. . . . Avoid financial involvement with the Serpent Seed."[54]

Adding to the urgency of the racial god's commands, there is the perceived danger of the seemingly omnipotent servant of the seed of the serpent, the United Nations, which is moving toward "requiring that each person of pure blood . . . intermarry with another race."[55] In response, Identity believers and other racial extremists have been gathering "like Noah" in order "to build an Ark of Safety,"[56] heeding the call for the preservation of the white race in various parts of the country. The danger in this kind of withdrawal is that it may lead to a siege mentality; perceiving themselves as surrounded by a spreading evil, they may conclude that there is no choice but to fight.

A skewed evaluation of self-importance adds to the volatile isolationism. An example is evident in the writings of the "Chaplain" of the Missouri 51st Militia. In his monthly "Chaplain's Letter" he blames the corruption of the federal government on the "selfishness" of those who have an "extremely inflated opinion of [their] own importance." Yet immediately following these accusations, speaking of the "last days" and referring to "the times when the forces of evil are gathering to engage in one final battle with the power of God," he claims a privileged place for the 51st Militia: "You should know that I feel, very strongly, that the Missouri 51st Militia will have an important role to play in the events of these last days . . . of all the militias which have formed across our nation, the Missouri 51st Militia will prove to be one of the most pivotal of all."[57]

Along with inflated self-importance there are often skewed perceptions of support. One poll of 402 respondents from across Montana revealed that the vast majority of Montanans oppose the view of the militias and the Freemen. The cofounder of the Militia of Montana, John Trochmann, responded: "How can they be against us? We're for the Constitution of Montana and the Constitution of the United States."[58]

In addition to gathering to preserve the white race, some Identity communities would ideally institute the death penalty for race mixers and homosexuals.[59] And to escape the corrupt schools that are part of the conspiracy to destroy the white race, home-schooling is recommended and practiced: "Home educate your children and avoid the dangers of the Serpent Seed reaching the minds of your children."[60] Identity adherents strongly oppose abortion because they believe it is part of the conspiracy to exterminate God's chosen people, white Israel. The Jews, it is claimed, promote abortion in order to destroy white babies: "The abortion clinics, which have murdered nearly 15 million White babies in the last ten years, are almost exclusively Jewish."[61] At the very least, the new racial extremists' goals are preparation for the coming racial war and the preservation of the white race. But many have joined up with more ambitious goals: a white Aryan homeland in the United States and, eventually, the world. Hitler's foreign policy has not died, and in enclaves scattered throughout the United States the cry still echoes: *Lebensraum* (living space).[62]

7

WORLDWIDE HATE
FOR HUNDREDS OF YEARS

There is no absolute freedom in history; for every choice is limited by the stuff which nature and previous history present to the hour of decision.

—Reinhold Niebuhr[1]

Where did Identity come from? The tendency is to scapegoat one individual or a group of strangers. Since World War II the creation of National Socialism and the blame for Nazi atrocities have tended to focus on one man, Adolf Hitler. And during the Freemen standoff in Montana reactions of those from Jordan and from people who had family and friends living near the site of the standoff included accusations that Freemen leaders were "outsiders" who had imported the blight of lawlessness, insurrection, and racism into Garfield County.

The following histories, figures, and developments spanning three continents explore Identity's multifaceted roots. Through these roots, we catch glimpses into manifestations of our shared human condition.

BRITISH-ISRAELISM AND RACIAL SALVATION HISTORY

Most analysts claim that Identity began as British-Israelism. This is an oversimplification, but Identity theology did find its impetus for revision of the Hebrew Scriptures' salvation history (*Heilsgeschichte*)

from British-Israelism, an eccentric religious movement that origi-
nated in Britain in the 1700s and asserted that the Anglo-Saxon
inhabitants of Britain were part of the biblical lost tribes of Israel.
With anticipation of a coming millennium fed by chronic national
and religious instabilities, the possibility of Britain's playing a role
in the final scene of history was apocalyptically energizing.

The first known British-Israelite figure was Richard Brothers
(1757–1824), whose "revelations" concerning a hidden Israel
ignorant of its divine origins mark the initial appearance of British-
Israelism's central credo: the white race constitutes God's chosen
people, but most of that race does not know it.[2] A British-Israel
movement took shape a generation later around the writings of John
Wilson, "the father of the rediscovery of Israel."[3] In his *Lectures on
Our Israelitish Origin* (1840), Wilson claimed that the nations of
northern Europe had their origins in the migration of the lost tribes
of Israel. Among the empirical footprints that, for Wilson, led to
Europe was language comparison. He used word sounds of unre-
lated languages to come to the conclusion that "many of our most
common [English] words and names of familiar objects are almost
pure Hebrew."[4] Wilson foreshadowed Identity mutations by claiming
that the tribes of Judah, because of intermarriage, were inferior and
that the promises of God preeminently belonged to British-Israel.
More and more in pre-Identity theology the Jews would come to be
known as descendants of an evil Asiatic race called the Khazars.[5]
Wilson claimed Israel was dispersed not only among the British, but
also among the Germans, Italians, French, and Scandinavians. But
the British retained a special status because of claims that they were
the descendants of the tribe of Ephraim, one of Joseph's sons to
whom Jacob's birthright blessing had been given (Gen. 48:19–20).

The revisionist movement begun by Wilson was continued by
Edward Hine (1825–91), who claimed to be converted to British-
Israelism while hearing Wilson speak. Hine's differences from his
mentor may have been a sign of the times. While the German States
consolidated into a united nation and began to thrive, Hine
claimed that the lost tribes were to be found exclusively among the
British, and he related Germany to the ancient enemy of Israel, the
Assyrians. The British-Israel movement peaked in England in the
1920s, and though within thirty years it would mutate into Identity,
throughout the 1920s the movement differed significantly from
Identity in that adherents were, for the most part, supportive of the
British Empire; many Identity adherents advocate armed rebellion
against the government. And members of the early groups in

Britain espoused British-Israelite doctrine while often maintaining membership in mainline congregations. In Identity circles, by contrast, the mainline churches are part of the problem and their pastors are "agents of Satan."[6] Because British-Israelite adherents did not organize into a particular sect, no one was in place to watch over the development of the new salvation history and resulting doctrine. Later, Identity was able "to draw in equal measure from the traditional and the bizarre."[7]

British-Israelism in the United States

Though it is not known whether he was the first adherent in the United States, Joseph Wild, pastor of the Union Congregational Church in Brooklyn, was publishing British-Israelite pamphlets in this country by 1879. Wild concluded that if Britain fulfilled the role of Ephraim, the United States fulfilled the role of the tribe of Manasseh as heir to the blessings given Joseph's offspring (Gen. 48:17–20). A man who helped spread the U.S. brand of British-Israelism was a retired artillery lieutenant, C. A. L. Totten. Totten generated many British-Israel writings, including a periodical published until six years after his death in 1909, *Our Race: Its Origin and Destiny*. His reputation caught the attention of Edward Hine in England. In 1884 Hine sailed to the United States for a four-year visit, touring the northeastern part of the United States and into Canada with his lectures. One of Identity's main West Coast contributors who would prove to be a vital link for the dissemination of the British-Israel message into southern California was pastor of the East Side Christian Church in Portland, Oregon, Reuben Sawyer, who lectured extensively in the Pacific Northwest and western Canada in the 1920s. Highly significant for Identity would be Sawyer's involvement in the Ku Klux Klan. During Sawyer's time with the Klan (1921–24) and as Identity salvation history evolved, the Klan's pervasive anti-Semitism and racial Christologies won out and helped set the stage for the development of Identity in the 1930s and 1940s.

A New Englander, Howard B. Rand, dominated British-Israelism from the 1920s until the end of World War II. A lawyer and second-generation British-Israelite believer, Rand was committed to generating a national movement. He increased evangelistic efforts, published a British-Israel magazine, *Destiny*, which boasted fifteen thousand subscribers, and helped consolidate the movement under the Anglo-Saxon Federation of America in the 1930s. A key development during Rand's tenure included the absorption of more mainstream right-wing leaders and causes. A factor in the growth of his Anglo-Saxon Federation was the involvement of another committed British-Israelite, William J. Cameron, head of press relations for automobile mogul Henry Ford from the mid-1920s to the early 1940s, and editor of Ford's magazine, the *Dearborn Independent*. Highly significant for the development of Identity doctrine was the publication of a series of anti-Semitic articles in the *Dearborn Independent* between May 1920 and January 1922, which made available to a large U.S. audience a fraudulent document describing the Jews' plans to take over the world, *The Protocols of the Learned Elders of Zion*.

British-Israelism Mutates into Identity

By the late 1930s British-Israelism experienced developments both geographically and doctrinally that led to Identity. Crucial themes emerged including charts of racial origins, the accusation that the Jews were literal children of Satan, the increasing role of the biblical character Cain, and wide-sweeping conspiracy theories.[8] The blossoming of Identity tendencies in the 1930s and beyond owed much to an evangelist from Wichita, Kansas, Gerald Winrod. He venomously attacked nonwhite races in his journal the *Defender Magazine*, which by 1934 had 100,000 subscribers. In 1934 he traveled to Germany, met with leading officials of the pro-Nazi church, and upon his return praised the Nazi regime and distributed its literature.[9] For its part, the Nazi propaganda arm World Service (*Welt-Dienst*) recommended Winrod's literature.

More than anyone else, Wesley Swift was responsible for combining Identity's salvation history, including a demonic anti-Semitism and Aryan Christology, with political extremism. He moved to the Los Angeles area in the 1930s, attended British-Israel's Kingdom Bible College, and founded his own church in Lancaster, California, in the mid-1940s, the Church of Jesus Christ, Christian.

Eventually, a unifying figure emerged through whom the metamorphosis of Identity can be traced to its contemporary leaders, a man who moved to Los Angeles in the early 1950s, the son of a Wisconsin pastor, Gerald K. Smith.[10] The racial movement into which Smith was grafted was undeniably Identity in orientation. Smith shaped and modestly unified Identity on the West Coast by cementing it to anti-Semitism and pushing in the political sphere an agenda informed by Identity. He organized the Christian Nationalist Crusade in 1947 and began an extensive speaking tour.

Echoing today's conspiracy theorists, Smith fed a growing assault on international cooperation and held a "Conference to Abolish the United Nations" in San Francisco in 1953.[11]

An Identity figure who entered the public scene after 1950 was a retired lieutenant colonel who served on General Douglas MacArthur's staff during World War II, William Potter Gale. Most significantly, in the early 1970s, Gale, along with Henry "Mike" Beach, founded the Posse Comitatus (Power of the County), based on the belief that the county government is the highest authority in the land and that the county sheriff and his posse are charged with enforcing the "Organic Constitution" and "God's laws." Although the Posse was not strictly an Identity movement, Gale tied the Posse to Identity extremism.

Identity figures such as James Wickstrom and perhaps the best-known Identity figure still active in the 1990s, Richard Girnt Butler, played dominant roles in the Posse's development. Butler, a Lockheed engineer who claims to have had a life-changing experience while listening to Wesley Swift preach, moved to Idaho in 1973, where he, like Swift, established his own Church of Jesus Christ, Christian. In addition to the church, he started the most publicly visible organization of the Identity movement, Aryan Nations, both of which are housed on a guarded compound in Hayden Lake, Idaho, where Aryan Nations congresses annually attract racial extremists from across the country.[12]

Since the shoot-out between Randy Weaver and federal law enforcement officers at Ruby Ridge, Idaho, in 1992, there has been an eruption of new Identity groups closely tied to the so-called militia movement. Activists in the new movement come from every corner of the well-established racist right. The militia movement, with its Identity ties, took further root after the 1993 Bureau of Alcohol, Tobacco and Firearms (BATF) raid on the Branch Davidian compound in Waco, Texas. The February 1994 passage of the Brady Law, which placed a five-day waiting period on all hand-gun purchases and required background checks, fed the fire of resentment. Currently, the militia movement and its relatives, the Constitutionalist, Sovereign Citizen, and Patriot movements, serve as vehicles for the spread of a racial salvation history.[13]

NAZISM'S ANTI-SEMITISM AND ARYAN JESUS

In eighteenth-century Germany, an ideology called the Volkish movement based on connections between a nation's language, land, culture, and history and a nation's race was evolving. By the end of the nineteenth century, the Volk had blossomed into a worldview that called for the termination of an encroaching modernity and the extermination of inferior races. Heading the list of those who could never be part of the Volk were the Jews. Adolf Hitler would declare at the height of this movement, "There cannot be two Chosen People. We are God's people."[14]

Combining medieval anti-Semitic stereotypes with ideas from the eighteenth-century Enlightenment and a new emphasis on classical arts, popular ideas about beauty and ugliness became regarded as windows to the interior race-soul. Toward the end of the eighteenth century, philologists concentrated on linguistics to uncover the roots of race. Many concluded that Sanskrit, imported from an Asian "womb of the world" by the migration of Aryan ancestors of the Anglo-Saxons, was the basis of all Western languages.[15] At the same time, with the Enlightenment's passion to define humankind's place in nature, the science of the races arose. This Volkish movement developed rapidly in Europe, notably blossoming in Germany into a Germanic faith, and eventually triumphing over all other ideologies.

The dualistic Identity world, where white warriors battle the Satanic Jews, has significant similarities with the division of the European population into Aryans and Semites, a distinction that by the end of the nineteenth century was widely embraced. At first, descent from Adam, a shared language before the Tower of Babel (Gen. 11:1–9), and the place of the cradle of humanity as the Judean countryside were generally accepted. But a complex interaction between different brands of nationalism and racial science resulted in conflicting claims. The Gauls, Franks, Goths, Celts, Germans, Normans, Teutons, and Romans vied for distinction as the pinnacle of creation.[16] As political, economic, and cultural crises wracked Europe, apocalyptic overtones were attached to the criteria of language and race. The growing conviction that the future of humankind depended on the preservation of the Anglo-Saxons was later echoed by Hitler: "Should he [the Aryan] be forced to disappear, a profound darkness will descend upon the earth, within a few thousand years human culture will vanish and the world will become a desert."[17] With the help of propagandists of a growing Aryan myth, during the second half of the nineteenth century, the division between Aryan and Semite was accepted as fact by the majority of educated Europeans, and the Aryan was often confused with the Christian people as a whole since Christianity was regarded as the "most genuine form of Aryan religion."[18]

With the Aryan myth as a driving force, ironically, before the First World War, France rather than Germany seemed the leading candidate for the success of a National Socialist movement. For example, Edouard Drumont (1844–1917), influential in popularizing National Socialism, became a widely read author and activist. One of his fourteen books (1886), which sounded the alarm that the Jews were responsible for national degeneration, sold more than a million copies.[19] French National Socialism took particularly deep roots in French-controlled Algeria where, for the mixed population of French, Jews, and Muslims, the tension of living together was a fact of daily life. The success of the Algerian National Socialists at the polls in the 1890s foreshadowed the Nazis' rise to power. And Max Regis, elected mayor of Algiers in 1897, called upon Algerians to "water the tree of liberty with Jewish blood" and, together with a city council of supporters, attempted to drive Jews from the city.[20]

If France's National Socialists are not enough to avoid scapegoating Germany as the birthplace of modern racism, England had its own racial prophets. Scottish anatomist Robert Knox (1798–1862), for example, claimed "race is everything, civilization depends on it" and spread his racial ideology through public lectures in many British cities.[21] An Austrian example was Georg von Schonerer, who especially between 1881 and 1907 fought against "alien" influences, including the Jews. For Schonerer, Christian baptism of Jews made no difference since "the filthiness lies in the race."[22] As Germany sought *Lebensraum* (living space), preexistent anti-Semitism in Romania, Hungary, Poland, and Arab North Africa and the Middle East proved fertile ground.[23] With this sweeping survey the danger of scapegoating a few "fanatics" is avoided and the mention of three key figures is placed in the context of a vast chapter of Western racial thought.

Gobineau, Lagarde, and Chamberlain

In an atmosphere where Europeans were being compared to the children of Abel and people of color to bloodthirsty children of Cain,[24] racial determinism was perceived by many as the main power in history.[25] A popular comprehensive racial theory took shape in the writings of Arthur de Gobineau, a French diplomat (1816–82),[26] who, when he published his work in 1854, developed ideas that had been fermenting for more than a half century: "The racial question overshadows all other problems of history . . . it holds the key to them all."[27] In addition to citing the most widely accepted anthropology and physiology of his day, Gobineau borrowed ideas on his history of the races from the book of Genesis, asserting that it dealt exclusively with the white race. Gobineau argued that Aryans were the purest race and must remain pure because "the basic organization and character of all civilizations are equal to the traits and spirit of the dominant race."[28] But, Gobineau asserted, as a result of expansion and conquest, Aryans had become contaminated and were doomed: "The white species will disappear from the face of the earth. . . . Winter is coming and you have no sons!"[29] Though Gobineau was not particularly anti-Semitic in his racism, by 1894, the German stage was set for the dissemination of Gobineau's ideas with an anti-Semitic twist.[30] Gobineau was disappointed with the initial reception of his work in France, but his friend Tocqueville assured him that his book "would return to France, above all by way of Germany," a chilling foresight.[31]

A prophet of antimodernity and of a new "Germanic religion," who helped shape Volkish thought in the late nineteenth century and left a legacy of de-Judaized Christianity and an Aryan Jesus, was Paul de Lagarde (1827–91).[32] Lagarde, an educator, received an honorary doctorate from the University of Halle and joined the faculty of Göttingen as professor in 1868. Rejecting traditional Christianity, which he viewed as corrupt beyond recovery, Lagarde set out to discover the "original faith," a Germanic religion cleansed of Jewish influences. He spread international conspiracy theories and thought Jews should be "exterminated as quickly and as thoroughly as possible."[33] Lagarde's popularity as a racial thinker increased after his death, and he was invoked as typifying the Volkish patriot. The likes of Ernst Krieck, National Socialist theorist of education, and Hitler's official ideologist Alfred Rosenberg were disciples of Lagarde's work. And at the height of the activity of the Nazi extermination camps in 1944, an anthology of Lagarde's work was distributed.[34]

The Volkish movement was attracted to the half-German Houston Stewart Chamberlain because of his hopes for a glorious future for Aryans. Seeing the debate over Jewish emancipation heating up, Chamberlain left the study of botany and devoted himself to writing. In his work *Foundations of the Nineteenth Century* (1899), and building on Gobineau and Lagarde, Chamberlain developed a theodicy pitching German against Jew. For Chamberlain, like the battles between Jesus and the devil revealed in the Bible, the German and the Jew epitomized opposites racially and ethically. Only one of the planned three volumes of *Foundations* was ever completed, but this twelve-hundred-page work launched Chamberlain into the limelight as an "apostle and founder of the German future."[35] Chamberlain's formulations were welcomed in the chaos of the postwar Weimar Republic in Germany and led the deposed Kaiser Wilhelm II to thank him for pointing "the way of salvation to the Germans and to all the rest of mankind."[36] By 1934 Chamberlain's book had gone through twenty-four large printings. His was an eclectic combination of Volkish thought and "Christian revelation," and he proclaimed an Aryan Jesus who could not possibly be Jewish.[37]

Chamberlain's influence on British and U.S. soil is easy to trace. The English translation of *Foundations* (1910) was reviewed by newspapers, professors, and politicians, and some were supportive of his work. Even Theodore Roosevelt was moved to read and comment on the work. As early as the 1880s Chamberlain was known well enough to be able to turn down invitations to lecture at Yale and Johns Hopkins University. Given the wide readership, one can imagine the success of *Foundations* in racial extremist circles.[38]

Toward the Final Solution

In an atmosphere charged with the ideology of Gobineau, Lagarde, and Chamberlain, racists asserted "good racial stock, not economic expertise, was essential to the continual vitality of the German race."[39] Such concerns resulted in the establishment of the German Anthropological Society (1871), resolved to gather statistics on all skull shapes in Germany. Notably, the society decided to focus its study on differences between Jewish and Christian children. From this research, craniologist Georges Vacher de Lapouge would later conclude, "The conflict of races is now about to start openly within nations and between nations. . . . I am convinced that in the next century people will slaughter each other by the million because of a difference of a degree or two in the cephalic index."[40]

This "Jew count" foreshadowed the singling out of German Jewish soldiers in 1916 to test the accusation that, due to inferior character, they avoided front-line duty during the war. Jewish stereotypes "took on metaphysical dimensions that had no connection with reality,"[41] religious forces were co-opted to strengthen the negative Jewish stereotype, and a Germanic faith continued to evolve. At this point differing from Identity theology, the Hebrew Scriptures were discarded and the Christian Scriptures salvaged from "foreign" influences. Following Lagarde and Chamberlain,

Jesus was remade into a German Aryan. Many in the church pledged allegiance to the Third Reich and openly supported its cause. Not until 1934 did some organized church resistance begin, but never did the majority of the clergy join in.

Volkish racial theories were disseminated through Germany's educational systems, and teachers passed on the German faith to the generation that would be involved in World War II. For example, teacher and activist Hermann Ahlwardt in 1890 published *The Desperate Struggle between the Aryan Peoples and Judaism*, in which he asserted that disposing of the Jews was the answer for lasting freedom for the Volk. Karl Eugen Duhring (1833–1921), who taught for a time at the University of Berlin, published *The Jewish Question as a Problem of Racial Character and Its Damage to the Existence of Peoples, Morals, and Culture* (1880), in which he claimed that there "is no sin, no failing for which the Jewish race is not held responsible," and which by 1901 had gone through five editions.[42] Motivated by fear that Jewish conspirators were infiltrating German schools, Hermann Lietz pioneered the boarding school movement and displaced the study of the Hebrew Scriptures with German medieval history. Such schools and the young people who passed through them inspired the German Youth Movement's allegiance to the Volk. Started as a hiking club for boys in Berlin, the movement quickly spread over northern Germany, and by 1911 had 15,000 members; by 1913–14, 84 percent of local chapters had adopted resolutions excluding Jews.[43]

Adolf Hitler transformed the anti-Semitism of an established Volkish movement into a political vehicle for his rise to power. Racism became the official German government policy on January 30, 1933, when Hitler became chancellor of the Reich. Promises to give new life to the nation were tied to the Jewish question. Hitler not only believed in the conspiracy laid out in the Protocols; he had the means to defend the nation against the mythical Jewish threat. In April Hitler approved an official boycott of all Jewish businesses.[44] As the Nazi government solidified its position, the Nuremberg Laws of Jewish exclusion (1935) put into policy the ideology of the Volk and punished Jews for being Jews. In September 1935 a complete list of Jews living in Germany was compiled, an action that prepared the way for the final solution of Jewish extermination.[45] Between 1933 and 1935 more than four hundred laws and decrees addressing the Jewish question were enacted in the Reich.[46] In January 1938, Hitler made it law that every male Jew's name was to be Israel, and every female's Sarah. In the eyes and minds of the Reich, they were all alike. In March 1938 Jewish religious congregations were deprived of legal protection.[47] And on November 9–10, 1938 riots were instigated (since then known as *Kristallnacht*, The Night of Broken Glass), that resulted in the destruction of about 7,000 Jewish businesses, the murder of nearly 100 Jews, the incarceration of about 30,000 Jewish males in concentration camps, and the destruction of nearly every synagogue in Germany.[48]

Aryans needed to put other races in their place but also needed to be purged of weaknesses, and the law safeguarding the Reich against hereditary sickness proclaimed on July 14, 1933, set the stage for the practice of euthanasia, a prelude to Jewish extermination.[49] In September 1939, Hitler gave increased authority for a euthanasia program. In the same year every asylum in Germany was ordered to report the condition of all patients, and the parameters of a "mercy death" were determined.[50] There was only one condition that did not have any loopholes; all Jewish patients were to be killed. Because many asylums were located in urban areas, nearby relatives and friends became suspicious of so many sudden deaths, and the public outcry resulted in the cessation of the program. Approximately 70,000 people were killed, at first by gunshot and then by a means that portended things to come, in gas rooms disguised as showers.[51]

In the spring and summer of 1941, orders to carry out the final solution were passed on by word of mouth and then in written orders on July 31, 1941. Jews had already been segregated into ghettos and deported to detention camps. Deportation took place in ways that added to the horror. Human beings were transported packed in cattle cars and upon arrival were evaluated for work duty; the "useful" were sent to work camps, and the others were gassed. Helped along by a highly organized, bureaucratic, industrial society, the mythical cosmic race war had actually taken shape.

Hitler's legacy has been clearly apparent in Arab nations such as Egypt, Iraq, Syria, Jordan, and Saudi Arabia—evidenced by the welcome granted fleeing Nazis, the series of jihads (holy wars) against Israel, the wide distribution of the Protocols along with Nazi literature, and virulent antipathy toward Israel coming from high levels of government.[52] The extermination of the Jews has been replaced with the extermination of Zionism, and Israel is seen not as a haven, but as a curse on the world. At the same time it is clear that in the United States, through Identity for one example, Hitler's legacy lives on.

ANGLO-SAXON MANIFEST
DESTINY AND AMERICAN NATIONALISM

The meeting of new Anglo-Saxon Americans and Mexicans in the Southwest in the mid-1800s and the eventual war with Mexico happened at a time when, more and more, racial superiority was used to justify expansionism. Into that atmosphere, while commenting on the "Mexican problem" and the annexation of Texas in 1845, politician and publicist John O'Sullivan coined the phrase "Manifest Destiny." He first used the phrase to criticize other nations for "checking the fulfillment of . . . manifest destiny to overspread the continent allotted by Providence for the free development of our yearly multiplying millions."[53] O'Sullivan used the phrase again while referring to the Oregon territory in his newspaper, the *New York Morning News*: "[it is] the right of our manifest destiny to overspread and to possess the whole of the continent which Providence has given us for the development of the great experiment of liberty and federated self government entrusted to us."[54] A week later Massachusetts state representative Robert Winthrop used the phrase while addressing Congress, and Manifest Destiny became a subject of debate for the following decades. Although the phrase was invented in 1845, it expressed the accumulated effects of an ideology of favored divine destiny that had been fermenting for more than two centuries.

Manifest Destiny and the Anglo-Saxon Myth

The English who settled in America in the seventeenth century brought with them a myth of a pure Anglo-Saxon past, and as royal pretentiousness grew, some people used claims of this untainted past to resist the British throne. Eventually, expansionists in America shared in the "discovery" that their achievements lay not in the institutions but in the blood. With the advancement west of the new settlers many analogically perceived God's kingdom moving west and America as the place from which the world would be renewed. Then came the move from America as promised land in the metaphorical sense to a view of the high destiny of America based on racial theories. These views were fed by the American Revolution; the young republic's defeat of England was, for many, a powerful sign that God had elected white Americans for special purposes.

For the most part through the 1700s, along with great pride in budding political institutions, the idea that other races could improve was influential. America may have been a guide for the world, but these views did not yet include domination or extermination of inferior races. But in the late 1700s and early 1800s the racial cast to American expansionism increased. For example, Senator Thomas Hart Benton, in his writings of 1818–19, described the Anglo-Saxons' movement west as "the disposition which 'the children of Adam' have always shown 'to follow the sun.'"[55] Along with claims concerning superior racial characteristics came claims of inferior racial characteristics. Thomas Jefferson expressed what many believed when he wrote in 1787 that "the blacks, whether originally a distinct race, or made distinct by time and circumstances, are inferior to the whites in the endowments both of body and mind."[56] By the 1840s the positive relationship between race and language was taken for granted, and nationality was determined on the basis of one's race.[57] This religio-mystical nationalism bloomed on American soil alongside and sometimes intertwined with British-Israelism and the anti-Semitism and racial Christology that burgeoned contemporaneously with the European Volkish movement.

America, the Promised Land

Amid a religious revival and the revolutionary cause, the colonists' sense of destiny under God was nationalized, God's redemption was temporalized, and American religious thinkers inaugurated an era of apocalyptic expectation blended with racism and patriotism.[58] In the late seventeenth and early eighteenth centuries, prophets of a coming millennium multiplied on both sides of the Atlantic, many of whom expected "a spiritual millennium in this world's flesh."[59] For example, Cotton Mather had no doubt that the capital city of the millennial kingdom would be in New England: "Many Arguments . . . perswade us that our glorious LORD, will have an Holy city in AMERICA, a City, the Street whereof will be Pure Gold."[60] Pastors as prominent as Jonathan Edwards speculated that the discovery of the New World and colonial expansion were signs of the imminence of a consummating millennial progression. He was convinced that Northampton, Massachusetts, was a hub for these developments: "If we consider the circumstances of the settlement of New England, it must needs appear the most likely, of all American colonies, to be the place where this work shall principally take its rise."[61]

While some believed in natural progress toward an earthly kingdom of God, another strain of thinkers, perhaps affected by the French and Indian War (1754–63) and the American Revolution, tended to think more militarily, creating a kind of cult of revolution.[62] In the theology of Joseph Bellamy, the first of Jonathan Edwards's successors, God seemed an anxious General eager to finish a battle: "When things have been ripening these five or six thousand years, and are now so nearly every way prepared for God, to get himself a great name in the total destruction of Satan's kingdom, can one imagine that God will let the opportunity slip?"[63] Samuel Harris, who would become professor of systematic theology at Yale, asserted that "any epoch in the progress of Christ's kingdom is liable to encounter violent and bloody opposition, and the advancement of Christ's kingdom may be in the midst of revolution. . . . In reference to this our Saviour said: 'I came not to send peace, but a sword.'"[64] Placing the theater of the last days in the United States caused an intranational dualism and set the battle between good and evil on American soil.

Manifest Destiny and the Racial Sciences

In the nineteenth century, especially between 1815 and 1850, the origin of humankind was largely taken out of the realm of theology and placed in the realm of the sciences. As the dangers of claims of heresy lessened, polygenetic theories were taken up in a variety of disciplines. Many who were willing to attempt to reconcile racial science with Christian orthodoxy did not perceive the equality of the races as an essential consequence. It was easy enough to assert that superiority and inferiority arose after the original creation. The scientific study of the races in the nineteenth century and its sociologically and popularly determined results were aided in large part by branches of study called anthropometry (anatomical measurement) and phrenology (study of the skull). Adherents to these forms of classification asserted a direct relationship between the hierarchy of races and body features and skull shapes.

By the 1840s the use of anthropometry and phrenology achieved great respectability in the scientific community. For example, Philadelphian physician Samuel George Morton used his vast collection of human skulls to study cranial structure, and in his works *Crania Americana* (1839) and *Crania Egyptica* (1844) he concluded that American Indians were decidedly inferior to the Caucasian race and that the Egyptians, with their superior civilization, had been Caucasian. Another figure who gained worldwide recognition in the 1840s for his work on the races was a leading physician and surgeon from Mobile, Alabama, Dr. Josiah Nott. Nott was zealous in his assertion of the polygenetic origins of humankind and radical black inferiority. He concluded that the advancement of civilization depended on the Caucasian race and advocated the extermination of inferior races. The close affinity between popular opinion and scientific findings should not be lost to those of us living in the so-called scientific age.[65]

Manifest Destiny Meets the Indians and Mexicans

Many who encountered the Indians in the seventeenth century originally thought in terms of improvability and acculturation. But after Jefferson's purchase of the Louisiana Territory in 1803, as the colonists expanded west, justification for the removal of the Indians was fed by racial theories. As in the case of the justification of black slavery, it was asserted that the fault lay with the Indians. Josiah Strong lent a messianic interpretation to the expendability of the Indians when he wrote, "It would seem as if these inferior tribes were only precursors of a superior race, voices in the wilderness crying: 'Prepare ye the way of the Lord.'"[66] At times it appeared that the problem was not that the Indians had failed to assimilate into white civilization but that they had succeeded. President James Monroe's secretary of war, John C. Calhoun, wrote on the success of the Cherokees in Georgia: "The great difficulty arises from the progress of the Cherokees in civilization. They are now, within the limits of Georgia, about fifteen thousand, and increasing in equal proportion with the whites; all cultivators, with a representative government, judicial courts, Lancaster schools, and permanent property."[67] After the election of President Andrew Jackson in 1828, it was made known through Jackson's secretary of war, John Eaton, that the Indians would not be protected in the southern states. In such an atmosphere Congressman David Levy of Florida stressed Indian atrocities and demonized his enemy: "Let us hear no more, I pray, from any quarter, of sympathy for these Indians. They know no mercy. They are demons, not men. They have human form, but nothing of the human heart. Horror and detestation should follow the thought of them. If they cannot be emigrated, they should be exterminated."[68]

Similar overt racial Anglo-Saxonism was brought to bear against Mexicans in the Southwest during the 1830s. After all, "to take lands from inferior barbarians was no crime; it was simply following God's injunctions to make the land fruitful."[69] Many people interpreted the Texas Revolution as a racial clash. Sam Houston, the two-term president of Texas, perceiving the conflict as one between the superior Anglo-Saxon and the inferior Mexican, asserted that there should be no concern for the population that inhabited northern Mexico and that they would "like the Indian race yield to the advance of the North American population."[70] Senator Robert J. Walker from Mississippi made Texas independence his cause, and in 1836, he called for the Senate to rejoice that "our kindred race predominated over that fair country, instead of the colored mongrel race, and barbarous tyranny, and superstitions of Mexico."[71] Extrapolating along the grain of the racial nationalism evident in settlement and expansion in the United States, Identity is not an imported blight but is in some ways indigenous.

8

OPPOSING THE
NEW RACIAL EXTREMISTS

*"The question is not whether we will be extremists, but
what kind of extremists we will be. Will we be extremists
for hate or for love?"*
—Martin Luther King Jr.,
"Letter from Birmingham Jail"[1]

In many parts of the world Identity extremism has advanced with
an apocalyptic passion fueled by the bleak prophecy that "the
Nordic race . . . will not see the year 2000" and the urgency that
comes with believing "we are living in the most momentous hour of
all ages" and approaching the consummation of the "warfare
between the seed lines."[2] Identity followers who believe they will be
subject to an "all-powerful world socialist superstate probably under
the auspices of the United Nations" are posturing for action. This
apocalyptic energy drives some Identity disciples into the world
"ready to conduct guerrilla warfare."[3] Others are evangelizing and
teaching their racial faith to their children, claiming they are teaching true Christianity. How can persons—religious or not—work
against more latent racism and extremist racist groups?

A RACIAL GOD GOES INTO THE WORLD

A racial god continues to infiltrate the world through Identity's
books, broadcasts, churches, and individual white warriors. For
example, July 1997 in Spokane, Washington, three white separatists

associated with the Identity congregation America's Promise Ministries in Sandpoint, Idaho, were given life in prison and up to $1 million each in fines for twice robbing a U.S. bank and bombing a newspaper building and a Planned Parenthood office. At the crime scenes the men left notes signed *Phineas Priests*.[4] In December 1997 a member of the Aryan Republican Army (ARA) committed to Phineas actions was the fourth to plead guilty for his involvement in at least eighteen armed bank robberies carried out for the race war between 1992 and 1996. Also pleading guilty of conspiracy was Mark Thomas, who has been a racist leader in Pennsylvania for decades and is a devotee of Phineas ideas. The Phineas symbol (a capital "P" with a horizontal line through it, which forms a cross) is painted near the entrance to his Identity church located near Hereford, Pennsylvania.[5] Another self-proclaimed Phineas Priest is serving a life term in Atlanta, Georgia, for a series of robberies in 1992 that he claims secured $2 million for the race war. The prisoner boasts: "We're willing to do virtually anything that has to be done because we are in a war, and those who are still active out there know that. . . . War rules are in effect, which means you can kill."[6]

Once again skewed biblical and theological images are brought to bear in the racial movement; Phineas is a biblical figure. Numbers 25:7–8 reads: "Taking a spear in his hand, [Phineas] went after the Israelite man into the tent, and pierced the two of them, the Israelite and the woman, through the belly." Phineas's violent actions against a Midianite woman and an Israelite man are used to justify violent behavior by racist Phineas Priests, who believe that the great sin punished by Phineas was race mixing. For them Phineas was "a great hero of the Bible," and this text proves that "a Race mixer is punished by a servant of God."[7] Such an interpretation inspired a book by Richard Kelly Hoskins entitled *The Vigilantes of Christendom: The Story of the Phineas Priesthood*, which advocates guerrilla holy war. The foreword sets the tone:

The story of the Phineas Priesthood . . .
As the Kamikaze is to the Japanese
As the Shiite is to Islam
As the Zionist is to the Jews
So the Phineas priest is to Christendom[8]

Groups such as Aryan Nations are intentionally attempting to "foster national and international Aryan solidarity."[9] Identity believers are urged to pass on their message to "seminary students, ministers, elders, church board members, Sunday School teachers, missionaries, and . . . state and federal officials."[10] One Identity evangelist exhorts his readers: "We must mold public opinion. We must stimulate interest by taking every opportunity to express our views on this critical subject. We must distribute literature on racial history in as large quantities as possible to our friends and neighbors for study . . . [and to] larger groups such as PTA's and civic clubs."[11] The racial movement is no longer something relatives and close friends share by word of mouth. To equip followers far and wide, Identity evangelists have the benefit of literally hundreds of World Wide Web sites,[12] glossy full-color publications, professionally produced documentaries, and the technology of television and radio to bring to bear.

At the millennium's turn, we are interacting with some second- and third-generation Identity believers nurtured on the racial worldview since childhood. Identity adherents who believe that hatred toward the white race "is locked into the very genes of Satan's Seed" are teaching their faith to their children.[13] Available are books such as *Kingdom Stories for Children,* which is "written from a British-Israel perspective" and is billed as one of the "excellent learning tools" in teaching the biblical history of the white race.[14] Stories in this book attempt to convince the young reader that all of God's promises in the Bible point to "Great Britain and her Dominions and colonies, and the United States" as the lands given to the white race, and that Britain was the "first country in the world to receive the gospel."[15] The racial god is reaching teenagers and young adults as well. Young Identity adherents given to loud music can "head-bang" and "body-slam" to the bands Skrewdriver and RAHOWA (an acronym for RAcial HOly WAr). The "good news" for this eclectic and widespread body of believers is that their god is going to deliver the world from sin and evil: the *sin* of race mixing, and the *evil* incarnate in the Jews and people of color.

GOD GOES DEEP INTO THE WORLD

God continues to go into the world through the church called to confess the truth of the gospel. To be sure, modern society is openly and pervasively pluralistic and relativistic with regard to "the truth." In many cases, and perhaps rightly so, people are cautious, if not belligerent, toward anyone who makes truth claims, even when the conversation is conducted with one eye on offensive racial extremism exhibited by the Montana Freemen or self-proclaimed Phineas

Priests. And in reaction to the "radical religious right," whose suspect theology often lacks depth and which most often makes the news, many view any theological discourse as an attempt by "radicals" to shape U.S. politics. Given the current tendencies to privatize and trivialize sincere religious devotion, another danger is that we concede that religious devotion, practically speaking, does not matter at all. It is merely a private matter to be lived out in the confines of church meetings and private devotions, with perhaps a bit of permitted talk about angels and higher powers.[16] This is a sensitive position to be in.

Long before the racial extremists began spreading their racial "gospel," the call went out to the church to proclaim God's promises for all. God has come and "lived among us" (John 1:14) and made God's self known. Jesus went public with this good news. We, in turn, are called to stake a claim in the world for God's promised coming kingdom and the sovereign loving reign of Jesus Christ. Insofar as this is the calling of every Christian, this constitutes the calling of the "priesthood" of all believers (1 Pet. 2:9). The drive by God is to go into the world, deep into the flesh, bearing witness to "the mystery hidden for ages" now revealed through the church (Eph. 3:7–12). For God this sending "of reconciliation" (2 Cor. 5:18–20) does not cease in this age. Those who believe in God's aiming at the world through Jesus Christ have a mandate to leave the "anaesthetizing security of stained-glass windows" and go into the world with God's intention to love, have mercy, and serve.[17]

Grace or Race?

As the core of Identity and the Christian gospel meet, the question arises, Is it grace or race? The meeting of these two faiths highlights that making claims concerning the Christian confession is necessary because what makes the church explicitly the *Christian* church is not always heeded or observed, or can be corrupted "by every wind of doctrine [and] by people's trickery" (Eph. 4:14). The Christian church on this side of the eschaton is constantly tempted to proclaim hope in names or things contrary to the confession or confuse the confession with another message, in the case of Identity extremists, a message fundamentally opposed to the Christian gospel.

The Christian church's confession depends totally on God's undeserved and unconditional *grace alone* given in Jesus Christ, which is for all people and is appropriated through *faith alone*, which clings to God's promises. The Reformation cry of faith alone was a polemic against those who might claim that with regard to salvation and our relationship with God, something is left to accomplish. With all of the controversial bridge issues used by racial extremists it is easy to lose sight of the church's specific calling and what actually is at stake. But the church's confession has one ground note, one theme, one center from which all else proceeds. This confession, cradled in the pages of the Bible, gives life to and determines the proclamation and action of the whole of the Christian church: "For there is no distinction, since all have sinned and fall short of the glory of God; they are now justified by God's grace as a gift, through the redemption that is in Christ Jesus" (Rom. 3:22–24).

Paul never pointed to a great Prometheus-like Aryan warrior, but decided to know nothing except "Jesus Christ, and him crucified" (1 Cor. 2:2), and not so that he could accuse someone of murdering Jesus, but because Christ died to reveal the depth of God's love for all people. And to the consternation of the righteous and the religious, and the racist and the Patriot, this Jesus whom Paul proclaims associated with sinners, prostitutes, tax collectors, those who collaborated with the "enemy" and beggars; he forgave sin and preached the kingdom of God for them. When he was resisted or heard complaint, he proclaimed, "I have come to call not the righteous but sinners" (Mark 2:17), and "I desire mercy, not sacrifice" (Matt. 9:13). Jesus' merciful inclusiveness and graceful crossing of perceived boundaries were too much for the world to handle, so the Son of God was banished from the world onto a cross. After three days the resurrection of Jesus Christ vindicated his merciful behavior and confirmed his words, way, and wounds as the will of God in the world.

The church must keep alert against other claims "out there," so the One who is served is the God who justifies the ungodly (Rom. 5:6). This is the Christian church's hermeneutic, the lens through which the church sees faith and life. In contrast to the new racial extremists the Christian church is extreme in a different way: embraced by and living out of the *extreme* love and mercy of God given in Jesus Christ, which is for all people. In short, the racial extremists say it is race; the Christian church says it is God's grace. One confession is centered in human "race," and the other is centered in Christ. This clearly reveals that the center is at stake and that the church must speak out. By looking at ways this confession has been brought to bear and has had an impact on communities in the first century and in the twentieth century, we learn from the witnesses who have gone before us.

A Prototype of the Church's Confession

Paul's letter "to the churches of Galatia" (1:2) was written sometime between 50 and 55 C.E. to churches he had visited and to which he had "announced the gospel" (4:13–14) at least one time before. What was at stake for Paul in writing to the Galatians was the confession of the church, namely, *the gospel of God's grace*. The small word "grace" sums up the salvation event for Christians. God's grace, for Paul, is not genetic or a hypothetical transaction, but a very powerful relationship. Grace is the historical manifestation of God in the life, crucifixion, and resurrection of Jesus Christ given for sinners. By grace, Paul meant that "when the fullness of time had come, God sent his Son, born of a woman, born under the law, in order to redeem those who were under the law, so that we might receive adoption as children" (4:4–5). That the core of the Christian confession was at stake for Paul is revealed in the emotion and intensity of the letter. But Paul also set about making the case for that on which the church stands or falls in the first century and today.

Apparently in Paul's absence other missionaries, the "circumcision faction," had been making the claim that all wanting to be adopted into the people of God through Jesus had to be circumcised, a kind of supplement to grace. Right away Paul called it a "different gospel" and was "astonished" that the church was "so quickly deserting" (1:6) God's unmerited grace. It was not the act of circumcision that was bewildering to Paul (Gen. 17:9–14) but the orientation of the claims of the missionaries that had a fundamental error in their direction. The missionaries were assuring their listeners what *they* could do to secure their place among the Christian community, what *they* could do to cope with the power of the flesh, and what *they* could do to fulfill the law.[18] But the gospel of God's grace finds its source in what *God* has done for sinful humanity.

After the letter's formal address, the first thing Paul offered was God's "grace to you and peace" (1:3). And then Paul built his case starting with the fundamental redirection that occurred in his life on the road to Damascus, a result of an encounter with the risen Christ (1:11–17; see also Acts 8:1–3; 9:1–19; 1 Tim. 1:12–16). As an example of the mercy of God, Saul the persecutor became Paul the proclaimer of Jesus Christ: "I was violently persecuting the church and trying to destroy it. . . . But when God, who had set me apart before I was born and called me through divine grace, was pleased to reveal his Son to me, so that I might proclaim him among the Gentiles, I did not confer with any human being" (1:13, 15–16).

Paul used his personal experience to reveal the *social* nature of God's decision to be for all. During Paul's meeting with the leaders of the Jerusalem church, grace alone (*sola gratia*) was the basis for unity and fellowship (2:1–9). Titus, Paul's companion on the trip to Jerusalem, though he was a Greek and uncircumcised, "was not compelled to be circumcised" (2:3). Circumcision would not be the basis of unity. Titus's and Paul's unity with the Jerusalem church and "the right hand of fellowship" (2:9) was founded on grace, *a unity in the gospel given amidst diversity.*

Further on, describing an incident at Antioch, Paul revealed that even the apostle Peter, a "pillar" of the Jerusalem church, was judged by the plumb line of grace (2:11–14). Considering the relationship between Jewish and Gentile Christians, Peter decided to withdraw from eating at the table with uncircumcised Gentile Christians; Paul's companion Barnabas followed Peter's example. When Paul discovered that church unity as it took shape in sharing meals together was imperiled by Peter, it was laid upon Paul to *make the good confession,* and Paul "opposed him to his face" (2:11). Paul was contending for "an evangelical unity"[19] expressed clearly in 3:28: "There is no longer Jew or Greek, there is no longer slave or free, there is no longer male or female; for all of you are one in Christ Jesus." In other words God's determination to be for the sinner depends on nothing inherent in the one being freely justified (male or female) or any type of social station (slave or free).

In the case of Identity, race implies divisions between people; baptism into Christ creates unity (3:27). It is not that ethnic, racial, gender, or social distinctions vanish, but that in the presence of God's justifying love given in Jesus these differences become irrelevant. This graceful irrelevance, however, does affect the distinctions listed. And for the relationship between Jew and Gentile and for the questions arising with respect to slavery and gender, the profound implications of unity in Christ are still being worked out today.[20]

The whole movement of the letter to the Galatians can be followed by "sniffing out" grace. At the beginning of chapter 3, Paul reminds the Galatians of their origins as adopted children of God by "believing what [they] heard" (3:2). God's people are those who share the *faith* of Abraham who believed the promises of God, "and it was reckoned to him as righteousness" (3:6). Christians are children of Abraham because "those who believe are blessed with Abraham who believed" (3:9). In chapter 4, with Paul's unusual handling of the story of the wife of Abraham, Sarah (Gen. 21:9–12), he proclaims God's radical grace by opening his hearers to identify with Sarah's offspring, Isaac, and to identify themselves, like Isaac, as "children of the promise" (4:28).

Identity adherents who believe that the Bible is God's revelation concerning the races are counterparts of those whom the apostle Paul was opposing, the "circumcision faction," and those turning to them for visible signs of security. If we extrapolate along the grain of one of Paul's exhortations, if people place faith in the law of genetics and live out of that racial worldview, they are not living in the grace of God; in the words of Paul they "have fallen away from grace" (5:4). The unity of the church is founded on one gospel of grace, not on the forces that naturally attract people and determine homogeneity, whether it is race, nationality, economics, lifestyle, or culture. Nor is unity found in what unites the paranoid conspiracy theorists, united as they are in their creation of objects of hatred and fear of being hated. Paul was seemingly exclusive regarding what, or rather who, constitutes the gospel of God's grace so that he might remove false conditions concerning communion in the church.

The Confessing Church in Nazi Germany

The history of the Confessing Church in Germany (1933–44) during the Nazi regime is a clear witness to the church impacted by racial extremism. It is helpful to note both similarities and differences between Identity extremism and the "German Christians." Similarities include nationalism being tied to race, virulent anti-Semitism and the dehumanizing of the perceived enemy, widespread conspiracy theories rooted in *The Protocols of the Learned Elders of Zion,* the use of controversial issues to gain a hearing, and a time marked by accelerated social, political, economic, and technological change.

In contrast, while Hitler acquired overwhelming popular support, Identity groups are a small minority. But Identity theology has moved *beyond* the theologians under Hitler by incorporating the Hebrew Scriptures. Other differences include the decentralized and eclectic nature of Identity believers and communities, and advanced technology available for the dissemination of their worldview. A difference holding hope is that an effective response is still an alternative. While many have already been profoundly and tragically affected by Identity, there is a sense in which we are still in the middle of it all.

The Confessing Church in Germany realized that the church's witness was imperiled by the distortions of the Hitler state and by the teachings of the "German Christians" that "in addition to God's revelation in Christ attested by Scripture there is a natural revelation in nature and history: in German blood, race, soil, and in the event of the National Socialist revolution."[21] To respond to the "German Christians" and Hitler's dictatorial powers, which became law on January 30, 1933, the First Confessional Synod of the German Evangelical Church convened May 29–31, 1934, in Barmen. One hundred thirty-nine delegates from Lutheran, Reformed, and United Churches and free synods believed they had been given a common confession to utter in a time of common need and temptation and unanimously adopted the Barmen Declaration authored by Reformed professor Karl Barth. The existence of different denominations was not perceived as an insurmountable barrier to claiming that the Confession of Barmen was speaking on behalf of the "one, holy, catholic Church."[22]

The Barmen Declaration taught first and foremost that a confession of faith confesses Jesus Christ as God's justification of the ungodly. God's graceful justification of the sinner (*any* human being) was exactly where the battle raged. In response to the "German Christians" who were proclaiming that God's salvation was being realized in the history of the German people, the Barmen Declaration confessed "Jesus Christ, as he is attested for us in Holy Scripture, is the one Word of God which we have to hear and which we have to trust and obey in life and death." As a result of this exclusive claim the church's people gather as "pardoned sinners," and the church must "render to all people the ministry of the proclamation of the free grace of God in Jesus Christ."[23]

Because of the exclusiveness of the confession of Jesus Christ, the Barmen Declaration encountered its greatest opposition both from the "German Christians" and from those who thought National Socialism was compatible with Christianity. But the genuineness of *any* Christian confession is reflected in this stupendous claim. And because of the constant temptation to add to the gospel of God's grace, a genuine confession of faith will not only proclaim but will also reject and condemn contradictory error, though never prematurely, abusively, or arrogantly. That is why the second paragraph of each article of Barmen began with the declaration: "We reject the false doctrine." As early as 1933 Dietrich Bonhoeffer and Karl Barth agreed that churches that accepted the "Aryan Paragraph" of Jewish exclusion must "be told directly, and at the same time publicly, 'Here you are no longer the Church of Christ.'"[24]

This aspect of a confession, that "confessional fellowship is based upon a positive and a negative factor," has often been regretted and protested with accusations of intolerance and lack of love. But the struggle for Israel and for the Christian church as it is expounded in the biblical texts is not so much whether there is a God; the issue is a struggle for the right God (Exod. 20:3; 1 Cor. 8:5–6). With this in mind it is illuminating to remember that "Hitler had no objections to Christians who confessed that Jesus is Lord; but he was enraged when they confessed that Jesus is Lord and Hitler is not."[25] The boundaries set by the Confessing Church are clearly revealed in an excerpt from a Memorandum personally delivered to Hitler on June 4, 1936, by the Confessing Church:

> When blood, race, nationality, and honor are . . . raised to the rank of qualities that guarantee eternity, the Evangelical Christian is bound, by the First Commandment, to reject the assumption. When the "Aryan" human being is glorified, God's Word bears witness to the sinfulness of all men. When, within the compass of the National Socialist view of life, an anti-Semitism is forced on the Christian that binds him to hatred of the Jew, the Christian injunction to love one's neighbor still stands, for him, opposed to it.[26]

The witness of Barmen is that both persons involved in the Christian church and disciples of racial extremism are held accountable as to whether they support or deny God's justification of the ungodly and include or exclude certain groups of people from free access to God's grace. It belongs to the heart of the gospel that "God shows no partiality" (Rom. 2:11), and for this reason neither can the communities who gather in God's name show partiality, wherever or whoever they may be.

The Social Implications of the Gospel

The gospel calls for and creates an evangelical unity grounded in the love of God for all people; justification by grace has profound social implications.[27] Though the gift of Christian community, because of sin, can become a burden, God's favorable judgment in Christ implies that the one justified is united with all those for whom Christ died. In being justified one is forgiven, and one enters into *the community of the forgiven* whose solidarity is found only in Jesus. Dietrich Bonhoeffer, writing during his call to run an "illegal" seminary during the Nazi regime, addresses the social implications of the gospel: "Christianity means community through Jesus Christ and in Jesus Christ. No Christian community is more or less than this. . . . We belong to one another only through and in Jesus Christ."[28]

The social dimension of the gospel should not be confused with mere tolerance or indifference. God is surely out to destroy sin, death, and the devil. And the love given in grace pushes toward expression in some tangible way. For example, at the Lord's Supper, grace destroys barriers and brings about unity in all kinds and levels of human diversity, including racial diversity. Also, this social dimension sends people out into the world seeing its creatures and creation as the beloved of God. Just as in the negative sense death is the great equalizer that ruthlessly levels distinctions between persons and stations in life, the death of Jesus Christ is equally for all.[29] In contrast to this social dimension of God's promises, Identity extremists stand with Jonah who was angry when God spared the Ninevites (Jon. 4:1–4), the older son who resented the loving embrace of the father welcoming the prodigal home (Luke 15:25–32), and the laborers who were angry with the landowner's generosity to the late-coming workers (Matt. 20:1–16).

The Confessing Church in Germany has often been accused of the tragic shortcoming of primarily being concerned with preserving its own existence and falling short in its witness against Nazi atrocities. Without minimizing this accusation or the confession of guilt made by the church in the *Stuttgart Confession* immediately following the war, this is not the whole story of the Protestant or Roman Catholic churches. The church struggle in Germany, especially after 1937, saw its pastors imprisoned, its passports confiscated, preaching prohibited, seminaries closed, and books and periodicals banned. At times, the Confessing Church failed to remain faithful to Barmen and present a unified witness against the Hitler state. But the Confessing Church was by no means entirely mute. One memorable document that witnessed to the gospel and related social and political issues was the personal Memorandum to Hitler mentioned earlier.[30] The Memorandum, written out of "anxiety for the souls entrusted to the Church," exposed the pagan character of the Hitler state and "openly condemned racialism, anti-Semitism, concentration camps, secret police methods, violations of the ballot, oaths of allegiance contrary to God's Word, the destruction of justice in the civil law courts, and corruption of public morals." Arthur Cochrane helps us realize the profundity of the Memorandum:

No action taken by the Confessing Church in the twelve
years of the conflict between Church and State is of com-
parable significance. Ten leading men of the Confessing
Church here opposed a totalitarian State with utter frank-
ness and without any personal security. They spoke God's
testimonies before kings and were not ashamed (Ps.
119:46). They had to put up with being forsaken, dis-
avowed, and maligned even by those who like them bore
the name of Christian. . . . And the evangelical Church may
be glad and thankful that in the midst of its confused and
often grievous history this testimony was made—to the
honor of God and the blessing of men.[31]

Against the wishes of the Confessing Church Council this
Memorandum appeared in the foreign press before it was known in
Germany, and National Socialists and "German Christians" labeled
it traitorous. This did not prevent the Confessing Church from distributing about one million copies of the Memorandum as a
message read from the pulpits of about three-quarters of the ministers of the Confessing Church. (Unfortunately, the Memorandum
was not even heard of in many areas.) The three men who were
responsible for the well-intentioned early release of the
Memorandum—Werner Koch, Ernst Tillich, and Dr. Friedrich
Weissler—were arrested during October and November 1936 and
placed in concentration camps. Koch was released in December
1938, and Tillich in 1939. Weissler died in Sachsenhausen on
February 19, 1937, a martyr of the Confessing Church.[32] Weissler's
solidarity with the world God so loves (John 3:16) reveals that the
role of the church in society can never be accurately evaluated
according to the standards of the world because its Christ was crucified, its strength is suffering love, and a strong Christian witness
may be perceived as weakness.

What About God's Laws?

Proclaiming Jesus Christ as the beginning and end of the
church's confession does not mean that all of the laws we live under
that operate as command or demand, limitation or restraint, are
bad. By no means (Rom. 6:1–2). But Barmen was faced with a situation where God's law was being confused with racial-biological
laws; the National Socialists believed the purity and dominion of the
German race were pursued with the sanction of divine law.

Barmen's witness concerning the law was that any state that wields the law "in the as yet unredeemed world" exists only "by divine appointment for the task of providing justice and peace" and should in no way be confused with Jesus' saving significance. In contrast to the "German Christians" and today's new racial extremists who look for God's salvific revelation in the history of the Adamic white race, "history is where God is defied" and is the realm in which is displayed "the progress of the condition of hardness of heart."[33] In this vein Pastor Asmussen, addressing the Synod of Barmen, wrote:

> We experience just like other people the beauty of God's creatures and their demoniacal character, the heights and depths of history that occurs under God's government of the world. But what we fear more than death is the fact that God's creatures and events in history lead us into temptation, as they have led all men into temptation in the course of history. [The "German Christians"] became heathen when they succumbed to the temptations to seek God without Christ from and in the creatures and events. Whenever that happens, whether under a pagan or Christian guise, there exist man's own wisdom, his self-righteousness, self-sanctification, self-redemption. Other lords than Jesus Christ, other commandments than his commandments, acquire dominion over us. They offer their services to us as saviors, but they prove to be torturers of an unredeemed world.[34]

Once the church is rooted in the gospel, the law, which is also given by God, functions in its proper place—not to storm heaven's gates, but right here on earth, between neighbors, controlling chaos and ordering humanity's life together. Also, as long as we are *unable not to sin,* the law reveals our sin and drives us back to Jesus Christ for forgiveness. But only the gospel is a new kind of speaking. *Only the gospel makes Christians.*

The Church's Confession of Sin

A temptation facing those responding to racial extremism is that they dehumanize racial extremists as racial extremists dehumanize Jews and people of color. The church cannot do this, for it lives before God under the same judgment as they do. In making the confession of faith the church will realize its life comes from God's

Table 3. Church Decrees and Nazi Laws

Church Decrees	Nazi Laws
Prohibition of intermarriage and sexual intercourse between Christians and Jews: Synod of Elvira (306 C.E.).	Law for the Protection of German Blood and Honor prohibited intermarriage and sexual intercourse: September 15, 1935.
Jews are not allowed to hold public office: Synod of Clermont (535 C.E.) and the Fourth Lateran Council (1215 C.E.).	Law for the Reestablishment of the Professional Civil Service eliminated "non-Aryans from civil service" and prohibited their holding public office: April 7, 1933.
Burning of the Talmud and other Jewish books: Twelfth Synod of Toledo (681 C.E.) and during the Inquisitions in the thirteenth century.	Book burnings in Nazi Germany: May 10, 1933. Torah scrolls destroyed: November 9–10, 1938.
Marking Jewish clothes with a badge: Fourth Lateran Council (1215 C.E.). Revived by the Roman Catholic Church in Italy in the sixteenth century.	A yellow star is required for all Jews in the Greater Reich: September 1, 1939. Instituted in Poland: fall of 1939.
Jews are not permitted to obtain academic degrees: Council of Basel (1434 C.E.).	Law against Overcrowding of German Schools and Universities: April 25, 1933. Jewish schools for boys over age twelve closed: June 1941.

Adapted from Raul Hilberg, *The Destruction of the European Jews* (New York: Holmes & Maier, 1985), 10–11.

justification of the ungodly, and there is always deep and abiding need for the confession of sin, individual and collective; this need never fades into the background. While distortions of the gospel are exposed, you and I are faced with our own sin and need for forgiveness. We are part of the problem, and only God has the answer. A partial comparison of the Christian church's actions and those of the Nazi regime exposes humankind's predicament. (See table 3.)

One need not point to the institutional hierarchy as a source of the need for repentance. For example, even though the papacy issued the *Constitutio pro Judeis* in 1120 forbidding violence against Jews, which was endorsed by successive popes ten times from its issuance until 1250, among clergy and laity violence against Jews continued unabated.[35] And centuries later, the Reformation seemed to easily absorb a long history of demonization of the Jew. Since the second and third centuries, Jews have been accused of working in union with Satan for the destruction of Christendom. As the church established itself, it attempted to convince itself, the infidels, and Jews that it had superseded Judaism as the true faith, tragically, not so much on theological grounds or with humility, but with burnings and beheadings. Charges that the Jews were in league with the devil, guilty of crucifying Jesus, practicing witchcraft, carrying out poisonings, seducing Christian women, and conducting ritual murder were rampant in the Middle Ages and reached a peak in the post-Crusade centuries. Everything from the senses to the sciences gave "proof" of evil intent. One could smell a Jew since good spirits emitted a pleasant odor and evil spirits a foul odor. And Jewish doctors, the myth went, murdered Christians: "When they come together at their festivals, each boasts of the number of Christians he has killed with his medicine; and the one who has killed the most is honored."[36]

There has been a seemingly impassable chasm between the *mythical* Jew, the *theological* Jew, and the *actual* Jew. One could display analogous lists of behavior using individual churches' and church bodies' culpability in the suffering of races and religious and ethnic groups throughout the centuries. These lists are of use if they drive the church to Jesus Christ for mercy and love that melt hard hearts so that Jesus Christ can be seen in the world, especially as revealed in those who are "different." In recent years documents such as the Roman Catholic "We Remember: A Reflection on the Shoah" (1998) and "The Declaration of the Evangelical Lutheran Church in America to the Jewish Community" (1994) are vital teaching tools that can facilitate the awareness of the need for repentance and further work.[37]

A CALL TO THE CHRISTIAN CHURCH

The church as the "priesthood of all believers" is called to respond to racial extremism in all of the situations God has placed them, whether as plumbers, politicians, nurses, social workers, mothers, fathers, insurance agents, athletes, ranchers, grocery clerks, teachers, students, or retired people. This is the way (God, help us) God goes into the world to respond to such dehumanizing.

How is one to expose racial extremism and offer alternative visions for our lives together in a given context? There is no formulaic answer. Just as Christian living cannot be done authentically from a serene mountaintop, but is done by making one's way crawling through the thickets of the valley at midnight, so responses to racial extremism will be worked out in particular circumstances. One can prepare for ministry by studying and being with one's conversation partner (in this case, racial extremists in person or through their materials), but the loving thing to do may differ depending on the circumstances, on the gifts one has to offer, and on the responsibilities encompassed in one's vocation.

With opportunities presented to it, the church spreads the fragrance that comes from knowing of the grace of God (2 Cor. 2:14). While others may believe there is nothing they can do to respond to racial extremism, and while there will always be those who "tranquilize themselves with the trivial,"[38] the church trustingly presumes that God can use *all* its people, whatever their shortcomings and whatever their gifts.

A Call for Prayer

In contrast to Identity, looking through the lens of the Christian church's confession of faith, one will see a creation deeply loved by God and people for whom Jesus Christ died. Given God's graceful movement toward the world and trusting its "high priest" who is able to "sympathize with our weaknesses" (Heb. 4:14–16), the church is called to *prayer*.

The apostle Paul wrote to his "loyal child" Timothy, urging him that "supplications, prayers, intercessions, and thanksgivings be made for everyone, for kings and all who are in high positions, so that we may lead a quiet and peaceable life in all godliness and dignity" (1 Tim. 2:1–2). He called the prayers "right" and "acceptable in the sight of God our Savior" (1 Tim. 2:3). Jesus said, "Love your enemies and pray for those who persecute you" (Matt. 5:44). Christians (and Jews) are commanded by God to pray so that God might mercifully hear their prayers and attend to them (Ps. 50:15).

In response to the world's heaving and bucking, Christians are called to pray for public servants, asking God to bring down the oppressor and to guard and guide those who work for justice and peace. And Jesus gives us the hard command to pray for enemies and those from whom we differ most, and in turn, our hearts will be opened to all for whom he suffered and died. Dietrich Bonhoeffer wrote, "I can no longer condemn or hate a brother for whom I pray, no matter how much trouble he causes me. His face, that hitherto may have been strange and intolerable to me, is transformed in intercession into the countenance of a brother for whom Christ died, the face of a forgiven sinner."[39]

And with Jesus, the apostle Paul, and all the saints who have gone before us, we are called to pray for the church in all its diversity and wherever it gathers in suburban structures, storefront missions, prison and hospital chapels, huts and homes, stadiums and cathedrals, and all of the places the people of God spend their days.

A Call for Faithful Congregations

What is vital for the church's response to racism is having people connected to communities of faith given life by the gospel so that they may be freed to give their lives away in witness and service. In these mission outposts grounded in the good confession the church may be guarded from being "tossed to and fro and blown about by every wind of doctrine" including the Identity variety (Eph. 4:14). In these communities of faith the church worships, prays, gladly hears the proclaimed Word of God, gathers around Christ's table, studies the Word of God, and is equipped to be sent out into the world in Jesus' name. In contrast to those who serve a racial god, curse the world, and barricade themselves around and about with weapons and walls, "we hope for what we do not see" (Rom. 8:25) and go into the world ready to give witness to that hope (1 Pet. 3:15).

These leads given for the priesthood of all believers are essential in highly diverse areas where Caucasians, people of color, and Jews live close to one another. And the hope of the church is that the unity amidst diversity given with the gospel is reflected in diverse communities of faith. What also needs to be highlighted is ministry done in more racially and culturally homogenous regions from which the call is going out for Identity believers and other racial extremists to gather in a kind of Noah's ark fashion. Though they may not be present in our communities, our shared heritage with our Jewish brothers and sisters and God's calls for advocacy and solidarity with brothers and sisters of all colors and faiths can be clearly expressed through the proclamation of the gospel, public prayer, and social action.

For my stance, I was sued for $100 billion for speaking out on behalf of brothers and sisters in Christ and human beings who were not present to speak for themselves. The congregation I now serve has a banner hung on the exterior of one of its brick walls that reads "One Lord of All . . ." and extends a welcome in seven languages. The hope expressed in this proclamation is that the church, more and more, through its hospitality, worship, service, preaching, and potlucks will reflect the evangelical unity given as a gift of God.

Public ministers have a unique calling to respond to racial extremism. They are given the vocation of going public with the gospel. Consequently, public ministers are not gurus, "shrinks," optimists, or law or Sabbath enforcement officers, but are *public proclaimers*. If this office entrusted to the church is forfeited, the uniqueness and purpose of the public ministry can easily become clouded, can become limited to a private matter compatible with the flow of modern trends, and can turn into any number of functions perceived as filling a more urgent need. All of a sudden Christianity becomes a private religion, and the public minister exercises his or her "personal skills" as a private family chaplain, counselor, social worker, or really nice "people person" to whom everyone can relate. At this point the *public* aspect of the ministry is threatened.[40]

A pastor's congregation is obviously the first and most frequent *public* he or she has to engage. The use of sermon illustrations, Bible studies, prayers, and pastoral care addressing racial extremism with both the law and the gospel will serve congregations well. What also needs to be emphasized is the pastor's responsibility to bring the Word of God to bear in the larger community outside the walls of the meeting place of the congregation. Though the present inertia tends to drive the pastor and biblical-theological discourse inside the building, pastors need not wait for an invitation to seek out ways to engage the larger community in loving and compassionate ways and with clear gospel words and actions. And contrary to recent developments in the types of discourse taking place in the public sphere, it is the larger community's responsibility to engage in theological discourse. For example, it would be negligent or betray a lack of understanding by community leaders if an informed pastor was not invited, along with a law enforcement officer and a public official, to speak at community meetings addressing issues such as the activities of militias or similar groups. But given current trends, a pastor should not expect to be invited unless there is communication with community leaders exposing the underlying biblical-theological issues that inform recent tax protesting and antigovernment agendas.

If pastors are approached by representatives of some form of media,[41] whether it is television, radio, or newspaper, they need to be aware that most likely—and this is a reflection of the condition of the larger society—reporters may not know how to address biblical-theological issues; they may not know the Bible well enough to understand the things at stake unless they are stated simply and clearly and are repeated;[42] they may not even know the right questions to ask. Unless they are specifically religious editors trained in that area (something only larger newspapers may have), reporters are asked to cover a union strike in the morning, a drug-related story in the afternoon, and the militia movement in the evening. They may not have time to research the topic. And pastors are not called to speculate on the psychological makeup of an individual of interest to the media or the outcome of a standoff. But in any given situation pastors are called once again and faithfully to make "the good confession in the presence of many witnesses" (1 Tim. 6:12–13).

There are churches and communities going public with the good confession. In Noxon, Montana, a small town of about 350 residents and headquarters of the Militia of Montana, the forty to fifty members of the Noxon United Methodist Church issued a public statement called "A Christian Response to the Militia." The statement condemned "selective love and vengeful hate" and pointed to the biblical concepts of "redemptive love and sacrificial service, even to those, yes, especially to those who we call our enemy." The statement also warned against using fear, suspicion, and scapegoating as "social tools for organizing movements and seeking change."[43] And during the Freemen's time spent near Roundup, the *Roundup Record Tribune* allowed me to publish a three-part series of articles exposing the biblical and theological agenda of the Freemen and other Identity groups and going public with Christian responses and proposals for community life.[44]

Faith communities and the larger public will also be served well by work done on intentionally strengthening Jewish–Christian relations. Mutual service—but beyond that, understanding, compassion, and love—can be nurtured during the absence of highly turbulent situations so that when those times come, the bridges of life-giving relationships have already been strengthened. Building on the confession of the sins of commission and omission by those implicated in the Nazi atrocities for one example, the church, through its leaders, will reach out with humility to those from whom the Hebrew Scriptures, our roots, and Jesus come.

A Call for Confessional Humility

The faithful posture for the church in response to the church's sin and implication in the sin of the world should not be to believe nothing and to tolerate everything. The ideology of tolerance and relativity is a secular "covert religion" that believes it has answers to life's ultimate problems. One of secularism's profoundest beliefs is that the *historical process* is redemptive. But Reinhold Niebuhr, writing at the sunset of the Nazi regime, realized that "modern history is an almost perfect refutation of modern faith in a redemptive history."[45]

Belief in the *relativity* of all human perspectives, whether because of a profound skepticism or oversimplification, "stands on the abyss of moral nihilism and threatens the whole of life with a sense of meaninglessness . . . [and] creates a spiritual vacuum into which demonic religions easily rush" (Matt. 12:43–45). However, it would be well for those who hold to a confession of faith to consider the reasons for the sacrifice of religious meaning on the altar of a hollow toleration for the sake of communal peace. The deadly bigotry of various religious fanatics, including the Christian variety, has sometimes left no other solution for the democratic state. But it does not take repentance to be religiously indifferent and universally tolerant, and one must ask "whether the health of a culture can be maintained upon the basis of such a shallow unity."[46]

The church is called to confess not the sin of holding fast to the good confession of the gospel but the sin of the people who cling to the confession and the sometimes atrocious ways the confession is held and given away. A hope holding promise for the world is that repentance and the confession of sin may lead to a much rarer *confessional humility* whereby people may hold ultimate religious convictions with a sufficient degree of humility as to live peacefully with those who differ from them.

That is, one may hold strong convictions and yet hold them (and give them away) with humility, love, patience, and gentleness (Gal. 5:22–23). This posture requires that "religious convictions be sincerely and devoutly held while yet the sinful and finite corruptions of these convictions be humbly acknowledged; and the fruits of other faiths be generously estimated." Here the needs of the church and the democratic society quickly and surprisingly converge; both democracy (for survival) and the church (for an authentic witness to the gospel) require *confessional humility*.[47]

A CALL TO ALL HUMANITY

The first thing every human being can do to respond to racial extremism is to discourage indifference. Jewish scholar Abraham

Heschel warns, "Indifference to evil is more insidious than evil itself; it is more universal, more contagious, more dangerous." Silence is a stance that makes it possible for the eruption of evil as an exception to be accepted as the rule. Hate talk that spreads in our communities is countered not by silence, but by a better, more life-giving kind of speech and accompanying actions. Humankind's sense of injustice is a poor analogy to God's, and God's anger pours forth from "the mystery of divine compassion"; one of the meanings of the anger of God is "the end of indifference."[48]

By not paying attention to what is happening regarding the contrast between Identity's public rhetoric and more hidden agendas, people may become complacent or sympathize with the bridge issues used to gain a hearing. And let it not be so, as Martin Luther King Jr. observed from his jail cell in Birmingham, Alabama, that "the white moderate . . . is more devoted to 'order' than to justice" and to a "negative peace which is the absence of tension" as opposed to a "positive peace which is the presence of justice." Related to this temptation, let it not be so that because the militia movement, compared to less well-armed city street gangs, is made up largely of "average white people"; they are not taken seriously as a threat to the American way of life.[49]

Billings, Montana, in 1993, stood as an example of a community mobilized for good. In November 1993 a group of racists threw a bottle through a window of the house of a Jewish family. A few days later they put a brick through the window of another Jewish house with a five-year-old boy in the room and smashed the windows of a Catholic high school that had "Happy Hanukkah" on its street sign. Many in the Billings community perceived these hate crimes as a community responsibility. The *Billings Gazette* printed, as a full-page advertisement, thousands of paper menorahs, and people all over the city cut them out and hung them in their windows as a sign of solidarity.[50]

In our vocation as citizens, creative discussion, debate, honest attempts at understanding, and the voter's booth are among the ways to promote, create, and maintain orders and structures that advance peace and justice. Such methods are not suggested to support the status quo. There will be times when the desire for justice and peace will lead to protest and radical reform. But presentations by racial extremist leaders tend to feed upon people's feelings of alienation, frustration, and perceived lack of power, offering clear-cut and easy answers and readily identifiable enemies when there seems to be nowhere else to turn and no one to blame.

In contrast, community members are called to work on and offer helpful and appropriate ways of addressing the challenges that face their neighbors' families, communities, and country. Demonizing an enemy is not the answer. Violence and intimidation are inappropriate responses to the complexity of our situation and need to be made unpopular and unwelcome. Though the challenge is formidable, we need to "move forward, and cannot go backward, in solving the problems with which higher forms of communal maturity present us."[51]

Besides Jews and people of color, those who have been particularly targeted by racial extremists' violent words and actions are elected officials, their coworkers, and families. The Indiana-based North American Volunteer Militia, when its Montana state leader was in legal trouble, threatened the lives of the Montana attorney general, members of the State Department of Fish, Wildlife and Parks, and the IRS. City judge Martha Bethel, because she presided over the traffic violation of a Montana Freeman, was threatened that her home would be shot up and she would be hanged. In Helena, Montana, opposition to changes in school district operations and land use regulations was so strong that law enforcement authorities advised public officials it was "not wise to have . . . addresses listed in the phone book or to have personalized license plates." And in Kalispell, Montana, county employees actually asked "if they can stay home for a few days after certain planning board votes," fearing that for some, shooting those you disagree with was an option.[52]

Certainly, as with any organization, among our public officials there are people who are not focused on the best interests of their communities. But those in office have been elected by the people; therefore, we should encourage, support, and protect them, and call them to task in appropriate ways. Residents of Ravalli County, Montana, in response to North American Volunteer Militia threats, posted signs supporting their elected officials, and a more formal proclamation signed by hundreds of residents was published in the *Ravalli Republic* calling for the cessation of threats. Federal employees are becoming the modern-day lepers in many communities, the "outsider" that community members are called to welcome with hospitality (Heb. 13:2).

The politicians who are cozying up to racial extremists and conspiracists must be held accountable. They must be reminded not to ignore the hatred and potential for violence from those perceived only as political allies; they must speak out when they see this hap-

pening, not for political advantage, but for the good of our communities. The acts of so-called Patriots and militia members are at times
obviously outside the realm of acceptable protest as one Montana
state representative found when her seven-year-old son was threatened after she agreed to carry a bill designed to make threatening
public officials or impersonating a public servant a felony: "Yell at me,
argue with me, don't vote for me, throw me out of office . . . but don't
threaten to kill my child or destroy my property because of the views
I take."[53]

As justified and reasonable as the plea for tolerance seems, this
work cannot end with a call for tolerance. Tolerance is not enough.
Jesus' cry of suffering love from the cross for all of humankind calls
for more than tolerance. At its best, mustering up tolerance fosters
a virtuous restraint. But the fact is I can still hate the one I tolerate.
Related to this, one of the most profound insights into our shared
human condition is realizing—better yet, confessing—that love for
one's neighbor cannot be conjured up, manufactured, forced,
coerced, legislated, or demanded. There is an infinite, unsurpass-
able gap between not killing our neighbor and actually loving our
neighbor—a gap that can only be bridged by an infinite love.

This work has exposed the theology, history, and agendas of
Identity racism. If these are ignored the response of the government, law enforcement, and the church might pass the racial
extremists like two ships in the night, or might collide with violent
and tragic results. The potential for violence depends not only on
Identity disciples, but also on the action taken by authorities
charged with keeping law and order. Once Identity racial extremism and its allied forces have been exposed, a more effective
response can be ventured. What shape this will take and what
resources are brought to bear for the government, law enforcement, and communities are left to be worked out. For the church's
part, an effective response is born out of its good confession: God's
justification of the ungodly given in Jesus Christ. And the church,
tied by God and through its people to all of the communities and
people that make up life together, will give itself up to the work for
justice and peace ventured by all.

NOTES

1. WELCOME TO ROUNDUP, MONTANA

1. Personal correspondence from Rodney Skurdal, March 3, 1994.

2. "Growing in Number, Hardening in Attitude: Patriot Groups Pose Continued Threat to American Public," *Southern Poverty Law Center Klanwatch Intelligence Report*, no. 86 (spring 1997): 4; Kevin Sack, "Hate Groups in U.S. Are Growing," *New York Times*, March 3, 1998.

Racial extremist groups not officially or uniformly holding to Identity doctrine are not ignored. Identity and non-Identity groups often perceive themselves engaged in the same battle. For example, the virulently racial National Alliance, National Socialist Vanguard, and World Wide Church of the Creator are not Identity groups, but their materials and rhetoric are often spread through Identity conduits. And not all groups of the Ku Klux Klan (KKK) officially hold to Identity doctrine, though some branches do. On the official Internet home page of the KKK it is asserted that "many Klan members and supporters are involved with the growing Christian Identity religion, which continues to unite the Christian Patriot Movement in the United States."

In Moscow, under the administration of Mayor Yuri Luzkhov, his idea of "Moscow for Muscovites" is virtually official policy, and there has been an increase in attacks on "foreigners" by neo-Nazi skinheads, which has caused the U.S. Embassy to issue two advisories cautioning African Americans and Asian Americans to be on guard. In Germany, the Office for the Protection of the Constitution, which monitors extremist groups, recorded 790 right-wing attacks in 1997 (a 27 percent increase from 1996), and there were 11,700 right-wing offenses recorded in 1997, 90 percent involving neo-Nazi propaganda, believed to be a postwar record. The antiforeigner German People's Union won 13 percent of the vote in state elections in Saxony-Anhalt, the extreme right's best showing since the war. See Inga Saffron,

"Racial Attacks Hit the Streets of Moscow," *Philadelphia Inquirer*, June 16, 1998, A1; Paul Geitner, "Neo-Nazi Attacks Increase in Germany as Right Wing Grows," *St. Louis Post-Dispatch*, May 7, 1998; Anne Thompson, "Right-Wing Showing Shakes Up Germany," *St. Louis Post-Dispatch*, April 29, 1998; Lev Krichevsky, "Skinheads Beat Russian Rabbi," Jewish Telegraphic Agency, May 11, 1998, Internet edition at <http://www.jta.org/may98/11-skin.htm>.

Note: Traditional or nonracist skinheads would have others know that not all skinheads are racist. In fact the racist variety are called "boneheads" by the others who are characterized by their music (a type of street punk), haircuts, clothes, and attitudes toward the predominant culture (see "NY Times and ADL Slander Skins Again," letter to the editor by Stephen Donaldson, *New York Times*, June 28, 1995; "Skinheads.Net FAQ," Internet edition at <http://www.skinheads.net>).

3. Clair Johnson, "Jury Hung on Some; Retrial Possible," *Billings Gazette*, July 9, 1998, 1A; Clair Johnson, "Jury Finally Gets Freeman Case," *Billings Gazette*, June 27, 1998, 1B; Clair Johnson, "Lawmen Waited While Freemen Ranted," *Billings Gazette*, June 4, 1998, 1A; May and December 1995 indictments from the Attorney for the United States in the United States District Court for the District of Montana, Billings Division.

4. Clair Johnson, "Trial for 14 Freemen Begins Today," *Billings Gazette*, May 26, 1998, 1A; Clair Johnson, "Freeman Trial Delayed As Defendant Is Taken Ill," *Billings Gazette*, May 27, 1998, 1A; Clair Johnson, "Two Freemen Plead Guilty, Jury Seated," *Billings Gazette*, May 28, 1998, 1A.

5. In the early 1980s Skurdal, a Montana native, having been injured on an oil rig in Wyoming, sued the local government using Freemen doctrine. He took the case all the way to the Wyoming Supreme Court before he lost. A traffic violation in 1992 began his more public battle with Musselshell County, which included a Citizens Declaration of War. At one point Skurdal had suits active in each of Montana's fifty-six counties, and three times was able to take traffic tickets to the Montana Supreme Court. In July 1993, the IRS seized his house and land to settle a $29,000 tax debt. Mark Pitcavage, "Every Man a King: The Rise and Fall of the Montana Freemen," *Militia Watchdog*, May 6, 1996, <http://www.militia-watchdog.org>.

6. Common Law Pleading in Common Law Court, Roundup, Mont., February 4, 1993, 2. Letter to the State of Montana Department of Revenue, Roundup, Mont., June 3, 1992. See Richard Abanes, *Rebellion, Racism, and Religion: American Militias* (Downers Grove, Ill.: InterVarsity Press, 1996), 29–40; "Against the New World Order: The American Militia Movement" (Portland, Oreg.: Coalition for Human Dignity, 1995).

7. The Freemen's theory of citizenship is "outdated and uninformed." Jonathan D. Varat, professor of constitutional law at UCLA, claims "the Fourteenth Amendment and subsequent Supreme Court rulings settled the question of whether federal authority prevails." Citizens of a state are not immune from federal regulation because they are also citizens of the United States. The Fourteenth Amendment did not create federal citizens;

the Constitution itself did. Militias, patriots, and Identity groups "forget that we fought the Civil War over the issue of state's rights. . . . The Union won" ("Constitutionalist Groups Misrepresent Both Fact and Law," Lawrence G. Wasden, *Advocate*, May 1996, 9; see also Abanes, *American Militias*, 34–37). Rodney Skurdal, Common Law Edict, Roundup, Mont., 1994, 14.

8. *Sheriff's Posse Comitatus* (Del City, Okla.: United Sovereigns of America, n.d.), 1, 12. August B. Kreis, *Posse Comitatus*, 1997. Internet edition at <http://www.webexpert.net/posse>. Mark Pitcavage, "Every Man a King: The Rise and Fall of the Montana Freemen," *Militia Watchdog*, May 6, 1996, <http://www.militia-watchdog.org>.

9. Pitcavage, "Every Man a King," 6; Clair Johnson, "Freeman Says Federal Laws Do Not Apply," *Billings Gazette*, June 24, 1998, 1A; Pitcavage, "Every Man a King," 13.

10. Skurdal, Common Law Edict, 13.

11. "Minister of Propaganda: Eugene Schroder," *Southern Poverty Law Center Klanwatch Intelligence Report*, no. 86 (spring 1997): 15.

12. See James Aho, *The Politics of Righteousness: The Idaho Christian Patriot Movement* (Seattle: University of Washington Press, 1990), 138–46. See *Calendar of Conspiracy: A Chronology of Anti-Government Extremist Criminal Activity*, vol. 1, no. 3 (July 4, 1997), vol. 1, no. 4 (December 4, 1997), vol. 2, no. 1 (February 10, 1998). *Militia Watchdog* Internet edition. See Affidavit by Rodney O. Skurdal (Roundup, Mont., September 14, 1992) in which two highway patrolmen, "two foreign agents," were sued for $1 million; "Ohio Policeman Kills Driver of 'Militia' Car," *Billings Gazette*, June 29, 1995; "Report: Freemen Checks Found in Car of Slain Militia Member," *Billings Gazette*, April 8, 1996; Mark Pitcavage, "Flashpoint America: Surviving a Traffic Stop Confrontation with an Anti-Government Extremist," *Militia Watchdog*, April 1998, Internet edition.

13. Names have been changed to protect identities.

14. *The Watchman* 18, no. 2 (spring 1995): 28–29.

15. Bill may well have been influenced by the language from the Identity book by Jack Mohr, *Satan's Kids* (St. Louis, Mo.: n.p., n.d.). Mohr writes, "The Jewish people are an assembling together of Satan's kids" (6).

16. "Seven Armed 'Freemen' Arrested Here Friday," *Roundup Record Tribune*, March 8, 1995, 1. Kenneth Stern, *A Force upon the Plain: The American Militia Movement and the Politics of Hate* (New York: Simon & Schuster, 1996), 172.

17. Ernest Becker, *The Denial of Death* (New York: Free Press, 1973), 2; Richard Harwood, "Death in the Twentieth Century," *Washington Post National Weekly Edition*, May 1–7, 1995, 27.

18. James Corcoran, *Gordon Kahl and the Posse Comitatus: Murder in the Heartland* (New York: Penguin Books, 1990), 8–19.

19. Abanes, *American Militias*, 50–51.

20. Denis Johnson, "The Militia in Me," *Esquire*, July 1995, 43; Becker, *The Denial of Death*, 5; "Letter from Birmingham Jail," in *God's New Israel:*

Religious Interpretations of American Destiny, ed. Conrad Cherry (Englewood Cliffs, N.J.: Prentice-Hall, 1971), 350. For example, see *Militia of Montana Catalog* (Noxon, Mont.: Militia of Montana, 1994); Clair Johnson, "'Things Got Terribly Greedy,' Freeman Says," *Billings Gazette,* June 17, 1998, 1C.

21. Becker, *The Denial of Death,* 33, 269.

2. GOD AND THE CREATION OF RACISM

1. Skurdal, Common Law Edict, 3; see also *Censored Bible Teachings* (Lynchburg, Va.: Virginia Publishing Company, n.d.).

2. Personal correspondence from Dan Gayman, December 14, 1995.

3. Pete Peters, pastor of the Laporte Church of Christ in Colorado, is an influential Identity figure. He is the self-proclaimed "evangelistic head of 'Scriptures for America,' a national outreach ministry dedicated to . . . revealing to the Anglo-Saxon, Germanic, and kindred (white) Americans their true Biblical identity" (*Scriptures for America Audio/Video Tape Catalogue,* iv). Peters' rise in stature was evident beginning in 1986 when his annual Rocky Mountain Bible Retreats attracted national racial extremist figures. Significantly, at Peters's 1992 Rocky Mountain Rendezvous held during the Randy Weaver standoff, the idea of paramilitary militias was revived.

4. Ben Williams and a group of followers established American Christian Ministries (ACM) based in Medford, Oregon, after a split in leadership following the death of Sheldon Emry, founder of America's Promise Ministries and Lord's Covenant Church (Phoenix, Ariz.), in 1985.

5. See *Articles of Faith and Doctrine for the Church of Israel, Diocese of Manasseh, United States of America* (Schell City, Mo.: Church of Israel, 1982), 9; Dan Gentry, *Death Penalty for Race Mixers (Is Prescribed in the Bible)* (Boring, Oreg.: Christian Patriot Association, n.d.), 2.

6. $100 Billion Freemen Lien against Pastor Jerry Walters, 9. Based on its use in chapters 5 and 9 of Genesis, the Freemen would need to change their interpretation of the word *image* (shadow, dark color), otherwise Seth would be black; this would be anathema for them: "[Adam] became the father of a son in his likeness, according to his *image,* and named him Seth" (Gen. 5:3). This is also true of the pronouncement after the Flood, when it is asserted that all the survivors are made in God's image: "in his own *image* God made humankind" (Gen. 9:6).

7. *Articles of Faith and Doctrine,* 9; *In the Image of God* (Merrimac, Mass.: Destiny Publishers, n.d.), 22, 54–55.

8. $100 Billion Freemen Lien, 7. In contrast to Identity's interpretation, a distinctive word encountered in the first creation account (Gen. 1:1–2:4b) is the verb "to create" (Hebrew *barah*), which in the Old Testament is used only to indicate the creative and redemptive activity of God. This reveals the creation of male and female as the climax of creation when it is used three times in verse 27 and makes untenable any Identity claims that this account represents a more generic or less crowning work of God because it lacks the distinctive nouns Adam and Eve.

9. *Freeman Edict,* 18; Gentry, *Death Penalty,* 6.

10. See *In the Image of God,* 54–61; M. K. Hallimore, *God's Great Race* (Harrison, Ark.: Kingdom Identity Ministries, n.d.). For the rise and spread of the racial sciences see Reginald Horsman, *Race and Manifest Destiny* (Cambridge: Harvard University Press, 1981), 43–61, 139–57; George Mosse, *Toward the Final Solution* (New York: Harper & Row, 1978), 77–93.

11. $100 Billion Freemen Lien, 6.

12. Ibid., 9. In contrast to Identity's interpretation, it is a widely held belief that two creation accounts have been brought together, Genesis 1:1–2:4a and 2:4bff. That there would be more than one creation account that enriches the scriptural witness should not shock readers of the Bible. There are four Gospels in the New Testament (Matthew, Mark, Luke, John), and this does not mean that Jesus lived four lives or that one of his lives was superior to another.

13. *Articles of Faith and Doctrine,* 8; *Kingdom Identity Ministries Doctrinal Statement of Beliefs* (Harrison, Ark.: Kingdom Identity Ministries, n.d.), 5.

14. Bertrand Comparet, *Your Heritage: An Identification of the True Israel through Biblical and Historical Sources* (Harrison, Ark.: Kingdom Identity Ministries, n.d.), 3, 36.

15. Sheldon Emry, *Heirs of the Promise: Abraham's Children* (Sandpoint, Idaho: America's Promise Ministries, n.d.), 25; J. H. Allen, *Judah's Sceptre and Joseph's Birthright* (Merrimac, Mass.: Destiny Publishers, 1917), 79.

16. *Doctrinal Statement of Beliefs,* 7; *Noah's Flood Was Not World-Wide* (Harrison, Ark.: Kingdom Identity Ministries, n.d.).

17. $100 Billion Freemen Lien, 6. See also *Doctrinal Statement of Beliefs,* 8–9; Gentry, *Death Penalty,* 2. In contrast to Identity's interpretation, the Hebrew wordplay between *adam* (man) and *adamah* (ground) emphasizes creatureliness, connection to the ground, and utter dependence on God. When God withdraws God's breath, man dies. Man is created from the earth (Gen. 2:7), must work the soil (3:23), and then returns to the earth when he dies (3:19). *Adam,* which can include reference to *ruddy, reddened,* or *to be red,* does not refer to the rose-red cheeks of a white Adam or to superiority, but points to the ground, the reddish brown earth (*adamah*) that Adam's complexion resembles, from which Adam came, and to which Adam will return. Humankind is made in the image of God, but made of dust as well. Adam is an earthling from the earth, a human from the humus.

18. Dan Gayman, *The Two Seeds of Genesis 3:15,* rev. ed. (Schell City, Mo.: Church of Israel, 1994), 7.

19. Ibid., 15–16, 291; William N. Saxon, *The Mask of Edom* (Merrimac, Mass.: Destiny Publishers, 1985), 17.

20. Gayman, *Two Seeds,* 192. See also *Doctrinal Statement of Beliefs,* 1.

21. *Doctrinal Statement of Beliefs,* 6.

22. Gayman, *Two Seeds,* 26.

23. Ibid., 210.

24. For a thorough treatment of the medieval conceptions of the Jew, see Joshua Trachtenberg, *The Devil and the Jews: The Medieval Conception of*

the Jew and Its Relation to Modern Anti-Semitism (New Haven, Conn.: Yale University Press, 1943).

25. Gayman, *Two Seeds*, 68; F. W. C. Neser, *The Serpent of Genesis 3* (Harrison, Ark.: Kingdom Identity Ministries, n.d.).

26. $100 Billion Freemen Lien, 7. In contrast to Identity's interpretation, that the serpent is not humanoid reveals that the origin of evil is not to be found solely in humankind (incarnational dualism) and is more than merely the individual will gone astray. At the same time, responsibility is not removed but is placed upon humankind. The emphasis is on the words the serpent speaks, clearly words that lead to temptation. The serpent claims to know God outside the concrete word of God that reveals the possibilities and limits of garden life. Eve did not have sexual intercourse with the serpent; the serpent's poison entered through Eve's ears.

27. *In the Image of God*, 29–30.

28. Gayman, *Two Seeds*, 67.

29. Saxon, *The Mask of Edom*, 22.

30. *Freeman Edict*, 3; see also David Lane, *Under This Sign You Shall Conquer: Identity* (Hayden Lake, Idaho: Aryan Nations, n.d.), 3–4. This pamphlet was written by David Lane of the Order, a group responsible for a string of western crimes in 1984. Lane, who was convicted of driving the getaway vehicle after the 1984 murder of Alan Berg, a Jewish radio talk-show host from Denver, believes he is a prisoner of war held by the Zionist Occupation Government.

31. Four hours of taped lectures by James Wickstrom, Posse Comitatus.

32. $100 Billion Freemen Lien, 7. In contrast to Identity's strictly sexual interpretation of Adam and Eve's nakedness, given the Hebrew conception of the essential unity of humankind, in the Old Testament nakedness is often associated with guilt before God. The prophet Jeremiah illustrates this point: "If you say in your heart, 'Why have these things come upon me?' *it is for the greatness of your iniquity that your skirts are lifted up,* and you are violated. . . . This is your lot, the portion I have measured out to you, says the Lord, because you have forgotten me and trusted in lies" (Jer. 13:22–26, emphasis mine; see also Hosea 2:2–3, Isaiah 47:3). After Adam and Eve ate from the tree of prohibition they clothed themselves (Gen. 3:7). Yet Adam indicates that he hid from God because he was *still naked* (3:10). What remained to be covered before God was their guilt. Despite the fact that Adam and Eve made clothes for themselves, their nakedness could only be relieved when God mercifully clothed them (3:21).

33. Robert Wistrich, *Hitler's Apocalypse: Jews and the Nazi Legacy* (New York: St. Martin's Press, 1985), 18.

34. Gayman, *Two Seeds*, 23; Neser, *The Serpent of Genesis 3*; *Articles of Faith and Doctrine*, 9–10.

35. Gayman, *Two Seeds*, 80.

36. Ibid., 121.

37. Ibid., 127–32.

38. $100 Billion Freemen Lien, 7; *In the Image of God*, 33.

39. Eustace Mullins, *The Curse of Canaan* (n.p.: Sons of Liberty, n.d.), 35. Jack Mohr, *Birthright or the Right to Govern* (St. Louis: n.p., n.d.), 2.

40. Gayman, *Two Seeds*, 212.

41. Arnold S. Leese, *My Irrelevant Defence: Meditations Inside Gaol and Out on Jewish Ritual Murder* (London: I.F.L. Printing and Publishing, 1938). See Trachtenberg, *The Devil and the Jews*, chapters 9 and 10.

42. *$100 Billion Lien*, 8.

43. Gentry, *Death Penalty*, 3; Saxon, *Mask of Edom*, 19.

44. This Cainite mythology can be traced to a variety of sources. Related to discussions about pre-Adamites, as far back as the 1700s it was suggested that the mark of Cain was black skin. This mythology prefigures later discussions on Cainite evil found in nineteenth-century Mormonism, early Mormon doctrine associating Cain with conspiracy and the nonwhite races. (See, for example, D. Michael Quinn, *Early Mormonism and the Magic Worldview* [Salt Lake City: Signature Books, 1987].) More recently and, in terms of effects on Identity, more directly, the attention given to Cain is in good measure credited to Mrs. Sidney Bristowe's life of Cain, *Sargon the Magnificent* (London: Covenant Publishing, 1927). (See also Barkun, *Religion and the Racist Right*, 164–67; Saxon, *Mask of Edom*, 19.)

45. *Yesterday: The Tribes of Israel, Today: The White Christian Nations* (Hayden Lake, Idaho: Aryan Nations, n.d.).

46. *Doctrinal Statement of Beliefs*, 5–6.

47. Gayman, *Two Seeds*, 219; Gentry, *Death Penalty*, 2; Mohr, *Birthright*, 4.

48. See for example Leon Poliakov, *The Aryan Myth: A History of Racist and Nationalist Ideas in Europe* (New York: Basic Books, 1974); Mosse, *Toward the Final Solution*.

49. Gentry, *Death Penalty*, 14.

50. For a pictorial rendition of "The Cradle of the Adamic Race" see Comparet, *Your Heritage*, 27.

51. *Noah's Flood Was Not World-Wide;* Pete Peters, *The Bible: Handbook for Survivalists, Racists, Tax Protesters, Militants and Right-Wing Extremists* (Laporte, Colo.: Scriptures for America, n.d.), 5; Bob Hallstrom, *The Law of Segregation* (Boise: Gospel Ministries, n.d.), part 1.

52. Gayman, *Two Seeds*, 222, 227.

3. GREAT NATIONS FOR WHITES ONLY

1. Sheldon Emry, *The Old Jerusalem Is Not the New Jerusalem* (Sandpoint, Idaho: America's Promise Ministries, n.d.), 25.

2. Emry, *Heirs of the Promise*, 27. Sheldon Emry founded the Lord's Covenant Church in 1967 in Phoenix, Arizona, and its outreach arm, America's Promise Ministries. His book, *Billions for Bankers, Debts for the People* (Phoenix: Lord's Covenant Church, 1984), identifies the U.S. government, the Federal Reserve, and world government as banker-owned and

controlled by Jews. He left a legacy of literature and tapes spread through the ministries of his heirs at America's Promise Ministries (Sandpoint, Idaho) and American Christian Ministries (Medford, Oreg.).

3. Sheldon Emry, *Paul and Joseph of Arimathea: Missionaries "to the Gentiles"* (Sandpoint, Idaho: America's Promise Ministries, n.d.), 23; see also Comparet, *Your Heritage,* 40–54; Emry, *Heirs of the Promise,* 18–19; *Articles of Faith and Doctrine,* 14; Pete Peters, *The Stolen Birthright and the Coming Destruction* (Laporte, Colo.: Scriptures for America, n.d.), 6; *Yesterday: The Tribes of Israel, Today: The White Christian Nations,* 2; *Censored Bible Teachings;* Karl F. Schott, *The Seed of Abraham* (Spokane, Wash.: Christ Gospel Fellowship Church, n.d.); Statement of Beliefs of the Covenant Vision Ministry, Australia, Internet edition at <http://www.rpi.net.au/frank/belief.htm>, 2; *Tare Time,* 2 of 15 (Wesley Swift, Sept. 26, 1965, available from Aryan Nations); Howard Rand, *Palestine: Center of World Intrigue* (Merrimac, Mass.: Destiny Publishers, 1949), 9.

4. For an example, see the map "The Reformation of Israel in the West: Israel's Tribal Migrations to 'The Appointed Place'" (Spokane, Wash.: Christ Gospel Fellowship Church, 1986).

5. David Duke, "My Indian Odyssey," Internet edition at <http//www.stormfront.org>. Then to Links. Then to David Duke, 6. See also Richard Kelly Hoskins, *Our Nordic Race,* rev. ed. (Lynchburg, Va.: Virginia Publishing Company, 1994), 22, 24.

6. Hallimore, *God's Great Race,* 2, 10. See also Hoskins, *Our Nordic Race,* 34–35.

7. Hallimore, *God's Great Race,* 17; Emry, *Heirs of the Promise,* 19.

8. Karl F. Schott, *America's Divine Destiny* (Spokane: Christ Gospel Fellowship, n.d.).

9. Gayman, *Two Seeds,* 153, 163.

10. See *Doctrinal Statement of Beliefs,* 5; see also Comparet, *Your Heritage,* 12–15; Allen, *Judah's Sceptre and Joseph's Birthright,* 220.

11. Gayman, *Two Seeds,* 164; Karl F. Schott, *Suppose We Are Israel, Does It Make a Difference?* (Spokane: Christ Gospel Fellowship, n.d.); Saxon, *Mask of Edom,* 10; Ted Weiland, *Could You Be an Israelite and Not Know It?* (Scottsbluff, Neb.: Mission to Israel, n.d.), 4–5.

12. Gayman, *Two Seeds,* 165. Claims run that the literal throne of King David was transported to Ireland by the prophet Jeremiah where it remained for about one thousand years, until 503 C.E., when it was transported to Scotland. From there it was removed to its present resting spot in England by Edward I in 1296 C.E. The conclusion is that the throne will no more be overturned (Ezek. 21:27) until it is removed to Jerusalem at the restoration of the kingdom of God to white Israel.

13. Gayman, *Two Seeds,* 176; Emry, *Paul and Joseph,* 29; *The Mystery of the Missing Bible Tribes!: The Real Diaspora* (Windsor, Canada: Canadian British-Israel Association, n.d.).

14. For the use of the term "Jew" in the Hebrew Scriptures, Apocrypha, and Christian Scriptures see Gerhard Kittel, ed., *Theological Dictionary of the*

New Testament, trans. Geoffrey W. Bromiley (Grand Rapids, Mich.: Eerdmans, 1964), 3:356–91.

15. Mohr, *Birthright,* 7.

16. Emry, *The Old Jerusalem,* 14–15.

17. Wesley Swift, *Was Jesus Christ a Jew?* Internet edition can be found at <http://stormfront.org/aryan_nations/jcjew.html>, 1.

18. Sheldon Emry, *Jesus Christ the Galilean* (Phoenix: Lord's Covenant Church, 1979), 8.

19. See Emry, *Jesus Christ the Galilean,* 26, 28; Swift, *Was Jesus Christ a Jew?,* 7.

20. Gayman, *Two Seeds,* 253; Mohr, *Satan's Kids,* 25.

21. Gayman, *Two Seeds,* 313; Emry, *An Open Letter to any Minister who teaches "the Jews are ISRAEL"* (Sandpoint, Idaho: America's Promise Ministries, 1987), 20.

22. See Emry, *An Open Letter,* 13; Malcolm Ross, *Christianity vs. Judeo-Christianity* (New Brunswick, Canada: Stronghold Publishing, 1984), 4–10; Gayman, *Two Seeds,* 245–48.

23. Walter Bauer, *A Greek-English Lexicon of the New Testament and Other Early Christian Literature* (Chicago: University of Chicago Press, 1979), 218.

24. Emry, *Paul and Joseph,* 28; *"Israel" in the New Testament* (Belfast: Open Bible Ministries, n.d.).

25. Gayman, *Two Seeds,* 32.

26. Ibid., 9.

27. Ibid., 24, 31.

28. Ibid., 9, 135, 151. See also *Doctrinal Statement of Beliefs;* B. P. Hawkins, *A Scriptural Study in Salvation* (Gloucestershire, Eng.: Britain's Background Publications, n.d.), 5, 12; *Articles of Faith and Doctrine,* 13.

29. Gayman, *Two Seeds,* 23, 32, 40. See also *Doctrinal Statement of Beliefs,* 3; Doctrinal Statement of Beliefs, the Lighthouse Internet edition link at <www.jubilee-newspaper.com>.

30. This author's emphasis. See $100 Billion Freemen Lien, 3; Comparet, *Your Heritage,* 19.

31. *Articles of Faith and Doctrine,* 25.

32. "Platform for the Aryan National State" (Hayden Lake, Idaho: Aryan Nations, n.d.), 5.

33. See Robert Crawford et al., *The Northwest Imperative: Documenting a Decade of Hate* (Portland, Oreg.: Coalition for Human Dignity, 1994).

34. $100 Billion Freemen Lien, 3.

35. Ibid., 11.

36. Ibid., 6.

37. *The Old Jerusalem,* 12; *A Scriptural Study in Salvation,* 16.

38. *Doctrinal Statement of Beliefs,* 7.

39. $100 Billion Freemen Lien, 25.

40. "Who Has the Right: God's Children or Satanists?" *Jubilee Newspaper* 9, no. 1 (Sept./Oct. 1996): 7.

41. Emry, *Paul and Joseph,* 24.

42. Ibid., 40. See also R. W. Morgan, *St. Paul in Britain, or, The Origin of British Christianity* (Muskogee, Okla.: Artisan Sales, 1860), 82–83.

43. Emry, *Paul and Joseph*, 40–41.

44. Hoskins, *Our Nordic Race*, 32.

45. Emry, *Paul and Joseph*, 15.

46. Alan Campbell, *"Israel" in the New Testament* (Belfast: Open Bible Ministries, n.d.), 7–8.

47. E. Raymond Capt, *The Traditions of Glastonbury* (Muskogee, Okla.: Hoffman Printing Co., 1996), 45. See also Morgan, *St. Paul in Britain*, 63–64.

48. See Morgan, *St. Paul in Britain*, 62; Eva Scott, *Kingdom Stories for Children* (Burnaby, Can.: Association of the Covenant People, n.d.), 46; Swift, *Was Jesus Christ a Jew?*, 5–6.

49. See also Mark 15:43; Luke 23:50; John 19:38.

50. Emry, *The Old Jerusalem*, 10.

51. Emry, *Paul and Joseph*, 1; Rand, *Palestine*, 19, 21.

52. Rand, *Palestine*, 11, 34, 90, 100.

53. Emry, *Paul and Joseph*, 19.

54. Comparet, *Your Heritage*, 11.

55. Emry, *The Old Jerusalem*, 17. See also Pete Peters, *A Scriptural Understanding of the Race Issue* (Laporte, Colo.: Scriptures for America, 1990), 1; New Beginnings—home page Internet site at <http://www.ioa.com/home/new_beginnings>; Mohr, *Birthright*, 12; *The United States in Prophecy* (Merrimac, Mass.: Destiny Publishers, n.d.), 2; Saxon, *Mask of Edom*, 11.

56. Allen, *Judah's Sceptre and Joseph's Birthright*, 227. See also Kenneth Goff, *America: Zion of God* (Boring, Oreg.: Christian Patriot Association, 1955), 30; *The United States in Prophecy*, 4.

57. Goff, *America: Zion of God*, 33–47.

58. See also *Judah's Sceptre and Joseph's Birthright*, 276.

59. Goff, *America: Zion of God*, 68.

60. Gentry, *Death Penalty*, 10.

61. Lane, *Under This Sign*, 10.

62. Emry, *Paul and Joseph*, 37.

63. Jack Mohr, *The Rapture: Scriptural Fact or Man-made Fiction?* Internet edition at <http://www.logoplex.com/resources/sfa/files/rapture.html>; on the rapture see also Swift, *Tare Time*, 5; Lane, *Under This Sign*, 10.

64. "The Declaration of Independence" (1996) from Aryan Nations Internet edition at <http://www.stormfront.org/aryan_nations/declar.html>.

4. THE PERSECUTION COMPLEX OF WHINERS

1. Gayman, *Two Seeds*, 229.

2. *Be Wise As Serpents* Internet edition at <http://www.bewise.com>.

3. Gayman, *Two Seeds*, 211; Rand, *Palestine*, 41; Ross, *Christianity vs. Judeo-Christianity*, 19; Emry, *An Open Letter*, 19; see also Richard Hardwood, *Did Six Million Really Die?* (available from Aryan Nations, Hayden Lake, Idaho),

which was actually written by Richard Verrall, the editor of *Spearhead,* a publication of a British neo-Fascist organization called the National Front.

4. Comparet, *Your Heritage,* 11.

5. Hardwood, *Did Six Million Really Die?,* 2.

6. Tom Blair, "The New Blasphemy," *Jubilee Newspaper* 9, no. 1 (Sept./Oct. 1996): 3.

7. The Institute for Historical Review in Newport Beach, California, was founded in 1978 by Willis Carto under the guise of devotion to "truth and accuracy in history," protection of "the First Amendment right of free speech," and the need to combat the "holocaust myth" used to finance Israel and vilify Hitler. *The Journal of Historical Review,* edited by Mark Weber and published six times yearly since 1980, spreads the theories that there were no gas chambers, no Nazi final solution, and that the deaths in concentration camps were caused by the Allies. Veiled under a scholarly veneer, the institute's agenda draws upon the work of "respected scholars" such as "best-selling British historian" David Irving (in Germany, Irving was convicted of crimes "against the memory of persons deceased" and banned from Canada, Germany, Australia, New Zealand, and Italy) and Arthur Butz, an electrical engineering professor from Northwestern University and author of one of the standard revisionist works, *The Hoax of the Twentieth Century.*

8. The Committee for Open Debate on the Holocaust (CODOH), in Visalia, California, with the help of an Internet site and a monthly newsletter, has recently focused resources on the "Campus Project," targeting students and professors. CODOH's Bradley Smith, who has been involved in Holocaust denial activities since the early 1980s, has placed advertisements in nearly one hundred college newspapers. More interesting and troubling than Smith's ads has been the response of college newspapers. Like deniers, many newspapers have claimed that freedom of speech mandated them to run the ad, forgetting that the article of the Constitution was written to prevent government's control over free speech, ignoring ways in which newspapers constantly choose material and neglecting advertisement policies that allow for censorship of racist, sexist, prejudicial, or religiously offensive material. Some newspapers repudiated Smith's claims to a free speech right to publish his ad. The *Harvard Crimson* called the ad "moronic and false" and "vicious propaganda . . . that has been discredited time and time again," and stated that to give Smith a forum was to "promulgate malicious falsehoods." The *University of Chicago Maroon* affirmed Smith's free speech rights but stated that it had "no obligation at anytime to print their offensive hatred." As Deborah Lipstadt has pointed out, the problem with publishing the ad along with a refutation is that Holocaust denial may be perceived as the "other side" of a legitimate debate. See Deborah E. Lipstadt, *Denying the Holocaust: The Growing Assault on Truth and Memory* (New York: Free Press, 1993).

9. In the early 1970s Zundel increased his publishing activities, including translating and publishing *The Auschwitz Lie* and *Six Million Swindle.*

Zundel's publication of *Did Six Million Really Die?* (1980) earned him special notoriety. In 1983 criminal charges were brought against Zundel, and in 1984 he was convicted under a statute making illegal the publication of "false news" that may cause injury. He was sentenced to fifteen months in prison. The conviction was overturned and a new trial ordered. Eventually, Zundel was acquitted of the charges because the false news statute was deemed unconstitutional. While traveling in Germany for a revisionist congress, Zundel was arrested by German authorities for "disparagement of the memory of persons deceased" and was convicted and fined. In 1994 he entered the world of cyberspace; there has been action taken to block Zundel's Internet site, Zundelsite. All the while Zundel was still being considered a "security risk" for Canada. In August 1996 Canadian officials ruled that Zundel could stay.

10. Lipstadt, *Denying the Holocaust,* 216.

11. The accusation about the six million came from President Nasser of Egypt in 1964. Wistrich, *Hitler's Apocalypse,* 188, 216–21.

12. Lipstadt, *Denying the Holocaust,* 9–10, 106. Austin J. App, professor of English at Lasalle College, is credited with formulating eight founding principles for the Institute for Historical Review and for Holocaust denial in general. They include the following (from Lipstadt, *Denying the Holocaust,* 99–100):

- The Nazi gas chambers never existed but were crematoriums used to destroy the bodies of those who had died of conditions brought on by Allied atrocities.
- The majority of the Jews who died under Nazi rule were in fact spies, saboteurs, and criminals.

13. Paul Hall Sr., "Mystery Babylon," *Jubilee Newspaper* 8, no. 3 (Jan./Feb. 1996): 19.

14. Gayman, *Two Seeds,* 23.

15. Ibid., 229; Emry, *An Open Letter,* 8–9.

16. See Saxon, *Mask of Edom,* 25; Gayman, *Two Seeds,* 232; Schott, *Suppose We Are Israel?*

17. Saxon, *Mask of Edom,* 25.

18. Gayman, *Two Seeds,* 235.

19. Saxon, *Mask of Edom,* 22.

20. Emry, *An Open Letter,* 13.

21. Gayman, *Two Seeds,* 265.

22. Ross, *Christianity vs. Judeo-Christianity,* 22; see also Francis Christen, *The Hoax of the Great Commission* (Medford, Oreg.: Serpent Slayers, n.d.), 59.

23. Gayman, *Two Seeds,* 253.

24. Ibid., 254.

25. Emry, *Paul and Joseph,* 31.

26. Gayman, *Two Seeds,* 26.

27. Lane, *Under This Sign,* 3.

28. See *Could You Be an Israelite?;* Emry, *Paul and Joseph,* 35.

29. Wesley A. Swift, *Reopening the Trial of Jesus Christ* (sermon given by Swift on April 15, 1962) (Harrison, Ark.: Kingdom Identity Publishers, n.d.).

30. Ibid., 35.

31. Sheldon Emry, *Who Killed Christ? A Treatise on the Bible Account of Jesus' Death on Calvary's Cross* (Phoenix: Lord's Covenant Church, n.d.).

32. Ibid., 17.

33. Ibid., 11, 14.

34. Ibid., 12–13.

35. Emry's biblical interpretation is completely false. First, the presence and activities of the Roman army are explicitly mentioned or implied throughout the Gospel accounts of Jesus' crucifixion. In the case of those who mocked Jesus and led him away to be crucified, the Greek military terms in the Gospels of Matthew (27:27) and Mark (15:16) are identical and very specific: "Then the soldiers [Greek, *stratiotai*] of the governor took Jesus into the governor's headquarters, and they gathered the whole cohort [Greek, *speiran*, a military term for one-tenth of a legion, or 600 soldiers] around him." After the use of "soldiers," there is no indication of a change of subject, and they are referred to with the use of the third-person plural, "They [the cohort of soldiers] stripped him and put a scarlet robe on him, and after twisting some thorns into a crown, they put it on his head . . . they led him away to crucify him" (Matt. 27:27–31; Mark 15:16–20). In addition, it is widely known that it was beyond the jurisdiction of the Jews under Roman authority to put anyone to death by crucifixion. Jesus died via a Roman method of capital punishment reserved for criminals, runaway slaves, and political rebels.

36. Lane, *Under This Sign*, 4.

37. Gayman, *Two Seeds*, 274. See also *Could You Be an Israelite?*, 4; Emry, *An Open Letter*, 11–12; Comparet, *Your Heritage*, 28; Hoskins, *Our Nordic Race*, 49–52; Gentry, *Death Penalty*, 11; Mohr, *Birthright*, 7–8; Mohr, *Satan's Kids*, 14.

38. Gayman, *Two Seeds*, 276.

39. Ibid., 277.

40. Mohr, *Satan's Kids*, 9.

41. Emry, *Paul and Joseph*, 33.

42. Emry, *Heirs of the Promise*, 25.

43. Lane, *Under This Sign*, 6.

44. Ibid., 8.

45. "Platform for the Aryan National State," Aryan Nations.

46. *$100 Billion Lien*, 12.

47. Gayman, *Two Seeds*, 279.

48. The Russian Revolution is mentioned frequently as an example of a Jewish plot against a "Christian" nation. See Ross, *Christianity vs. Judeo-Christianity*, 16–17; Mohr, *Satan's Kids*, 26–27; Emry, *An Open Letter*, 15; Dan Gayman, *The Duties of a Christian Citizen* (Schell City, Mo.: The Church of Israel, 1995), 322–23; Gary Allen, *None Dare Call It Conspiracy* (Rossmoor,

Calif.: Concord Press, n.d.), 40, 58–78; Lane, *Under This Sign*, 7, 29; Mohr, *Birthright*, 7.

49. See Abanes, *American Militias*, 73–130.

50. Gayman, *Two Seeds*, 350.

51. Sightings of "black" helicopters have been explained repeatedly. Even though the helicopters spotted are usually able to be identified as aircraft from the National Guard or the armed forces, they have evolved into symbols of the satanic New World Order (David Fenner, "General Says Guard Copters Cannot Be Marked," *Billings Gazette,* June 17, 1995, 2B).

52. See "Weather Theory Blowing in the Wind," *Billings Gazette,* June 16, 1995; Arlene Levinson, "Weird Theories Often Spring from Bad Luck," *Billings Gazette*, May 22, 1995, 1A.

53. Wistrich, *Hitler's Apocalypse*, 190, 213.

54. Mohr, *Birthright*, 10. See also Gayman, *Two Seeds*, 281–87; Emry, *The Old Jerusalem*, 24; Rand, *Palestine*, 47–49.

55. Rand, *Palestine*, 40.

56. Ross, *Christianity vs. Judeo-Christianity*, 3; "Jewish Control Over the Media," *Christian Defense League Report* (Arabi, La.), no. 187, 1–4, 22.

57. *$100 Billion Lien*, 25.

58. Evidence of the glue that holds many of the racial extremist groups together can be seen in the number of pages dedicated by the CPA (Christian Patriot Association, Boring, Oregon) in its 1997 book and tape catalog: "Christianity-Race-Religion" (fourteen pages), and "History-Conspiracy" (eight pages). Of the twenty-four sections in the catalog, these are the two largest.

59. Rand, *Palestine*, 40.

60. Stern, *A Force Upon the Plain*, 154.

5. FROM "JEWISH LIES" TO *THE TURNER DIARIES*

1. Taken from the work by Norman Cohn, *Warrant for Genocide: The Myth of the Jewish World-Conspiracy and the Protocols of the Elders of Zion* (Chico, Calif.: Scholars Press, 1981).

2. *Be Wise as Serpents*, Internet edition at <http://www.bewise.com>, 1; Rand, *Palestine*, 48–49.

3. Sergey Nilus, *The Protocols of the Learned Elders of Zion*, trans. Victor Marsden (n.p., n.d.), 11–64.

4. Cohn, *Warrant for Genocide*, 73.

5. Ibid, 26.

6. Ibid., xvii.

7. Abanes, *American Militias*, 141.

8. Cohn, *Warrant for Genocide*, 115.

9. Ibid., ix.

10. Adolf Hitler, *Mein Kampf* (London: Hurst and Blackett, 1942), 174; see Wistrich, *Hitler's Apocalypse*, 89.

11. Cohn, *Warrant for Genocide*, ix.

12. Abanes, *American Militias*, 143.

13. Ralph Lord Roy, *Apostles of Discord: A Study of Organized Bigotry and Disruption on the Fringes of Protestantism* (Boston: Beacon Press, 1953), 43–44.

14. Wistrich, *Hitler's Apocalypse,* 175, 177, 186, 204.

15. Swift, *Reopening the Trial,* 4–6; Gayman, *Two Seeds,* 281–87; Mohr, *Satan's Kids,* 3, 15–17, 31; Emry, *An Open Letter,* 20–21; Rand, *Palestine,* 47–49; Hoskins, *Our Nordic Race,* 50–51; Peters, *The Stolen Birthright,* 8; *Be Wise As Serpents,* Internet edition at <http://www.bewise.com>.

16. Lawrence Elliott, "This Lie Will Not Die," *Reader's Digest,* April 1995, 115–19.

17. Pierce has also published *Hunter* (1989), a kind of prelude to the racial revolution depicted in *The Turner Diaries* in which Oscar Yeager, a Vietnam veteran with a Ph.D., becomes repulsed by the decay of modern society and becomes a vigilante who kills interracial couples, Jews, and gays.

18. Andrew Macdonald (real name William Pierce), *The Turner Diaries,* 2d ed. (Hillsboro, W.Va.: National Vanguard Books, 1995), 34–35, 71.

19. Ibid., 23.

20. Ibid., 39–42.

21. Ibid., 102.

22. Ibid., 111.

23. Ibid., 150–51.

24. Ibid., 155; It seems the author is following Hitler's example here. In the early stages of the war Germany's foreign policy included intentionally exporting anti-Semitism through ideology, but also by the dispersal of Jews stripped of their property and assets so that all people would come to recognize "the danger which the Jews represent for the racial preservation of the nations" (Wistrich, *Hitler's Apocalypse,* 100–101).

25. *The Turner Diaries,* 162.

26. Ibid., 182.

27. Ibid., 199.

28. Ibid., 207.

29. Ibid., 211.

30. A letter written by Timothy McVeigh to the *Lockport Union-Sun and Journal* (Lockport, N.Y.), February 11, 1992.

31. Jonathan Alter, "Jumping to Conclusions," *Newsweek,* May 1, 1995, 55.

32. See Mark Eddy, George Lane, Howard Pankratz, and Steven Wilmsen, "Guilty on Every Count," *Denver Post Online,* June 3, 1997; Howard Pankratz and Steve Wilmsen, "Lawyer Admits McVeigh Did It," *Denver Post Online,* June 3, 1997; George Lane and Kevin Simpson, "Mixed Verdict on Nichols," *Denver Post Online,* December 24, 1997.

33. Howard Pankratz and Michael Booth, "Nichols Escapes Death Penalty," *Denver Post Online,* January 8, 1998, at <http://www.denverpost.com>; Stacie Oulton, "Experts Analyze the Decision," *Denver Post Online,* January 8, 1998; George Lane and Peter G. Chronis, "Nichols Wants New Trial," *Denver Post Online,* February 10, 1998.

34. *Time* magazine interview with Timothy McVeigh by Patrick Cole at the El Reno Federal Correction Institute, March 30, 1996. See also Howard

Pankratz, "'Turner Diaries' an Inspiration?" *Denver Post Online*, May 2, 1997.

35. Tom Morganthau, "The View from the Far Right," *Newsweek*, May 1, 1995, 36–39.

36. Stern, *A Force Upon the Plain*, 13–14.

37. Bill Morlin, "Devoted to Making Nation 'Ungovernable,'" *Spokane Spokesman Review*, December 29, 1996, Internet edition at <http://www.VirtuallyNW.com>.

38. Joseph A. Slobodzian, "Guilty Plea in Bank Heists by Hate Group," *Philadelphia Inquirer*, December 9, 1997.

39. "National Alliance: North America's Largest Neo-Nazi Group Flourishing," *Southern Poverty Law Center Klanwatch Intelligence Report*, no. 82 (May 1996): 7.

40. William Pierce, "OKC Bombing and America's Future," *American Dissident Voices*, Internet edition at <http://www.stormfront.org/stormfront/adv-okc.htm>, 2–3. See also Marc Fisher and Phil McCombs, "Going by the Book of Hate," *Washington Post National Weekly Edition*, May 1–7, 1995, 9.

41. "Crossing the Threshold: The Increasing Threat of Biochemical Terrorism," *Southern Poverty Law Center Klanwatch Intelligence Report*, no. 85 (winter 1997): 8–9; John Kifner and Jo Thomas, "Singular Difficulty in Stopping Terrorism," *New York Times*, January 18, 1998.

42. "D.C. Patriot Rally Attracts Groups from Throughout the United States," *Southern Poverty Law Center Klanwatch Intelligence Report*, no. 84 (November 1996): 17. See also Phil Linsalata, "Militias See Verdict as Confirmation of Conspiracy," *Detroit News*, June 3, 1997, Internet edition at <http://detnews.com>; Guy Kelly, "Militia Member: Bomb Victims Deserve Facts," *Rocky Mountain News*, February 24, 1996, Internet edition at <http://www.denver-rmn.com>.

43. See "Gulf War Illness: An Interview with Joyce Riley," *Jubilee Newspaper* 8, no. 3 (January/February 1996): 10–11; "Order Jubilation '96 Tapes!" *Jubilee Newspaper* 8, no. 5 (May/June 1996): 13. See also Pat Shannan, "'Closure' More Important Than Justice: Tim McVeigh Is Chosen Blood Sacrifice," *Jubilee Newspaper* 9, no. 6 (July/August 1997): 1, 8–9; Dave Barley, "Exposing the Gulf War Syndrome" (Sandpoint, Idaho: America's Promise Ministries), Internet edition at <http://amprom.org>.

44. See Gayman, *Two Seeds*, 354–56; Ross, *Christianity vs. Judeo-Christianity*, 11–12; Emry, *Who Killed Christ?*, 30; Emry, *An Open Letter*, 18–19; Leese, *On Jewish Ritual Murder*, 48.

45. Wistrich, *Hitler's Apocalypse*, 138–44. See Uwe Siemon-Netto, "Luther and Hitler: Friend or Foes?" *Dialog: A Journal of Theology* 35 (summer 1996): 188–92.

46. Eric W. Gritsch and Marc H. Tanenbaum, *Luther and the Jews* (Minneapolis: Fortress Press, 1995), 11.

47. Heiko Oberman, *The Roots of Anti-Semitism in the Age of the Renaissance and Reformation*, trans. James I. Porter (Philadelphia: Fortress Press, 1984), 96.

48. Ibid., 37.

49. Ibid., 39–40.

50. Ibid., 48.

51. Ibid., 101.

52. "That Jesus Christ Was Born a Jew," in *Luther's Works* (LW), American ed., vol. 45, ed. Walther I. Brandt (Philadelphia: Muhlenberg Press, 1962), 195–232; see 197.

53. Ibid., 199.

54. Ibid., 200.

55. Gritsch and Tanenbaum, *Luther and the Jews*, 13.

56. Ibid., 8.

57. "On the Jews and Their Lies," in *Luther's Works* (LW), American ed., vol. 47, ed. Franklin Sherman (Philadelphia: Fortress Press, 1971), 121–306; see 268–69.

58. Ibid., 275.

59. Gritsch and Tanenbaum, *Luther and the Jews*, 14.

60. See James Arne Nestingen, "Luther, Judaism, and Cultural Tolerance," *Dialog: A Journal of Theology* 35 (summer 1996): 169–70.

61. *On the Jews and Their Lies*, 6. Received from the Freemen, March 3, 1994.

62. LW, 47:191–92.

63. Nestingen, "Luther, Judaism, and Cultural Tolerance," 169.

64. Edwards, *Luther's Last Battles* (Ithaca, N.Y.: Cornell University Press, 1983), 208.

65. Gritsch and Tanenbaum, *Luther and the Jews*, 15–16.

6. USING POLITICAL ISSUES AS A COVER

1. "Authorities Having Trouble Communicating with Freemen," CNN Interactive, April 10, 1996, at <http://www.cnn.com>.

2. Some famous racial extremists started in the John Birch Society but moved on because the society was perceived as insufficiently militant or insufficiently anti-Semitic. The list of former Birchers includes Robert DePugh (later leader of the Minutemen), Gordon Kahl (later of the Posse Comitatus), Robert Mathews (later leader of the Order), and Willis Carto (later leader of the Liberty Lobby and founder of the Populist Party).

3. Johnson, "Freeman Trial Delayed As Defendant Is Taken Ill"; Clair Johnson, "Freemen, Judge Show Restraint," *Billings Gazette*, July 18, 1996, 1B.

4. "Freemen Renounce U.S. Government as 'Corporate Prostitute,'" CNN Interactive, April 9, 1996.

5. Leonard Zeskind, "Armed and Dangerous: The NRA, Militias, and White Supremacists," *Rolling Stone*, November 2, 1995, 59.

6. Goff, *America: Zion of God*. See also *The United States in Prophecy*.

7. $100 Billion Freemen Lien, 3. See also *Censored Bible Teachings*. Pete Peters, in *The Bible: Handbook for Survivalists* (7–9), also cites the biblical figure Gideon as "a tax protester" (Judg. 6:1–11).

8. Barkun, *Religion and the Racist Right*, 206.

9. A statement by Gordon Kahl, 1983 (four pages).

10. $100 Billion Freemen Lien, 20.

11. Clair Johnson, "'Freeman' Trial Can't Seat Jury," *Billings Gazette*, January 5, 1995. The Montana Criminal Syndicalism Act, recently used to prosecute extremists, was originally created to counter radical labor unionists during the First World War. The law, passed in 1918 along with a sedition act, was later adopted by the U.S. Congress. In 1921, Congress repealed the sedition act. In 1973, when the state criminal codes were updated, Criminal Syndicalism remained on the books. When William Stanton was convicted in February 1995 in Miles City and sentenced to ten years in prison, news accounts claimed Stanton was the first to be prosecuted under the statute (Ed Kemmick, "Roots of Syndicalism Law Go Back to Butte Troubles," *Billings Gazette*, September 4, 1995; Dennis Gaub, "Stanton Receives 10 Years," *Billings Gazette*, March 3, 1995, 1A).

12. *Freeman Edict*, 19.

13. CPA Book Publisher 1997 Catalog (Boring, Oreg.: Christian Patriot Association).

14. *Censored Bible Teachings* (pamphlet).

15. Stern, *A Force Upon the Plain*, 72; this section is adapted from pp. 107–18.

16. Pete Peters, *Everything You Wanted to Know (and Preachers Were Afraid to Tell You) about Gun Control* (Laporte, Colo.: Scriptures for America, n.d.).

17. John Branton, "Clark County Militia," *Columbian*, November 13, 1994, A1.

18. Roger Worthington, "Private Militias March to Beat of Deep Distrust," *Chicago Tribune*, September 25, 1994. For an overview on militia history and law in the United States see Mark Pitcavage, "New Militia FAQ Part Three: Militia—History and Law FAQ," *Militia Watchdog* at <http://www. militia-watchdog.org>; John Flesher, "Hard-Core Gun Activists Ready for Day When Arms Are Needed," *Los Angeles Times*, November 13, 1994, 32A.

19. Stern, *A Force upon the Plain*, 111, 113.

20. Ibid., 118.

21. "'Militia' Chief Predicts Violence," *Billings Gazette*, March 12, 1995.

22. See Sue Anne Presley, "Disabled Man Dragged to Death," *Washington Post*, June 10, 1998, A3; Sue Anne Presley, "Down a Dark Road to Murder," *Washington Post*, June 13, 1998, A1. For a comprehensive overview of extremist criminal activity see Mark Pitcavage, "Calender of Conspiracy," *Militia Watchdog*, Internet edition at <http://www.militia-watchdog.org>. Lee Hancock, "Ex-Con Says Man Plotted Racial Killing," *Dallas Morning News*, February 19, 1999; Lee Hancock, "King's Writings Cast Him as a Hero in Racial Conflict," *Dallas Morning News*, February 17, 1999.

23. Louis Beam, "Leaderless Resistance," Internet edition at <http://www2.cybernex.net/odin/misc-lr.html>, 3–4, 6.

24. Ridgeway, *Blood in the Face: The Ku Klux Klan, Aryan Nations, Nazi Skinheads, and Rise of a New White Culture* (New York: Thunder's Mouth Press, 1990), 88.

25. See Mark Pitcavage, "Aryan Nations Leader Enters Surprise Guilty Plea," Militia News Archives—*Militia Watchdog* at <http://www.militia-watchdog.org>; Slobodzian, "Guilty Plea in Bank Heists by Hate Group"; "Midwest Robber Caught," Associated Press, *Beloit Daily News*, May 25, 1996, Internet edition at <http://www.bossnt.com/596/1wis25.html>.

26. Charles Bosworth, "Illinois Man Sought Start of Race War," *St. Louis Post-Dispatch*, March 15, 1998, 1A; Charles Bosworth, "Two Plead Guilty of Weapons Charges Involving Extremist Group," *St. Louis Post-Dispatch*, May 15, 1998, 1B; Charles Bosworth, "One Gets Bail, 1 Doesn't in Alleged Terror Ring," *St. Louis Post-Dispatch*, May 13, 1998, 1B; Charles Bosworth, "Tapes Detail Violent Plans of Hate Group," *St. Louis Post-Dispatch*, May 6, 1998, 1A; Patrick E. Gauen, "Ex-Klan Leader Admits Guilt on Weapon Counts," *St. Louis Post-Dispatch*, April 28, 1998, 1A.

27. Barkun, *Religion and the Racist Right*, 231.

28. See Kevin Flynn and Gary Gerhardt, *The Silent Brotherhood: Inside America's Racist Underground* (New York: Free Press, 1989).

29. The Order, Declaration of War, Internet edition at <http://www.nidlink.com/fourteenwords/current.html>, 2.

30. Jeff Randall, "The New Militia," *Jubilee Newspaper* 8, no. 3 (Jan./Feb. 1996): 9.

31. Dan Gayman, *The Duties of a Christian Citizen: A Handbook on Christian Citizenship* (Schell City, Mo.: Church of Israel, 1995).

32. For an excellent discussion of contemporary racial politics see Barkun, *Religion and the Racist Right*, 199–223.

33. *Articles of Faith and Doctrine*, 17.

34. Gentry, *Death Penalty*, 11.

35. Clair Johnson, "Partial Verdict," *Billings Gazette*, July 3, 1998, 1A; Clair Johnson, "Freemen Sore Losers, Prosecutor Says," *Billings Gazette*, June 26, 1998, 1C; "Prosecuting Patriots around the U.S.," *Southern Poverty Law Center Klanwatch Intelligence Report*, no. 84 (November 1996): 6.

36. U.S. Department of Justice, "Robert Young and Frank Pepper Found Guilty," February 6, 1997. Though militia groups and Patriots distanced themselves from the Republic of Texas events, few can match the grandiosity of their claims. The Republic of Texas's common-law court levied a "judgment" of $93 trillion, payable in gold, against the United States, the Federal Reserve, the International Monetary Fund, and the Roman Catholic Church.

37. See Rodney Skurdal, Citizens Declaration of War, September 10, 1992, and Declaration of Citizenship, March 1, 1992. See also Declaration of John Ernest Trochmann, Sanders County Recorder's Office, January 26, 1992, 2–3; Public Notice Positive Identification of John Ernest Trochmann, Sanders County Recorder's Office, January 26, 1992, 2; Clair

Johnson, "'Wanted' Judge Takes Witness Stand," *Billings Gazette*, June 10, 1998, 1A.

38. See letter to Sheriff G. Paul Smith of Musselshell County, June 1994.

39. Rodney Skurdal, True Bill/Private Security Agreement against Dave's Towing-Exxon, Roundup, Mont., October 13, 1994.

40. Wynn Miller, "Montana 'Freemen' Clog Court System," *National Law Journal*, July 16, 1995, A9.

41. See Patricia Sullivan, "Militants Expensive for Counties," *Billings Gazette*, June 25, 1995, 1C.

42. "Declaration to Regain a National State," a Resolution published by Aryan Nations.

43. Corcoran, *Gordon Kahl and the Posse Comitatus*, 29.

44. Barkun, *Religion and the Racist Right*, 210.

45. Ridgeway, *Blood in the Face*, 169.

46. Elizabeth A. Rickey, "The Nazi and the Republicans: An Insider View of the Response of the Louisiana Republican Party to David Duke," in *David Duke and the Politics of Race*, ed. Douglas Rose (Chapel Hill: University of North Carolina Press, 1992), 60.

47. Lawrence N. Powell, "Slouching toward Baton Rouge: The 1989 Legislative Election of David Duke," in *David Duke and the Politics of Race*, 32.

48. Rickey, "The Nazi and the Republicans," 62–64.

49. Ibid., 68.

50. William B. McMahon, "David Duke and the Legislature: 'A Mouth That's Different,'" in *David Duke and the Politics of Race*, 120.

51. A term used by GOAL (God's Order Affirmed in Love) <http//www.melvig.org>.

52. Bob Hallstrom, *The Law of Segregation* (Boise: Gospel Ministries, n.d.), part 1.

53. Gayman, *The Duties of a Christian Citizen*, 49. See also E. R. Fields, *Interracial Dating/Interracial Marriage Right or Wrong?* (Marietta, Ga.: The Truth at Last, n.d.), 24; Pete Peters, *A Just Look at Racism* (Laporte, Colo.: Scriptures for America, 1990), 13.

54. Gayman, *Two Seeds*, 297–98.

55. Mohr, *Birthright*, 9.

56. *Articles of Faith and Doctrine*, 25.

57. Lawrence Watson, "Chaplain's Letter," December 20, 1996.

58. Patricia Sullivan, "University of Montana Poll: Most Montanans Oppose Beliefs of Militia Groups," *Billings Gazette*, August 2, 1995, 1A; John Halbert, "Study: Freemen Expected Public Support," *Helena Independent Record*, June 14, 1998, 1A.

59. Gentry, *Death Penalty*; Pete Peters, *Intolerance of, Discrimination Against and the Death Penalty for Homosexuals Is Prescribed in the Bible* (Laporte, Colo.: Scriptures for America, 1992).

60. Gayman, *Two Seeds*, 297.

61. Lane, *Under This Sign*, 6.

62. For more on the Nazis' foreign policy see Klaus Hildebrand, *The Foreign Policy of the Third Reich* (Berkeley: University of California Press, 1973).

7. WORLDWIDE HATE FOR HUNDREDS OF YEARS

1. Reinhold Niebuhr, *The Children of Light and the Children of Darkness: A Vindication of Democracy and a Critique of Its Traditional Defenders* (New York: Charles Scribner's Sons, 1944), 54.

2. Barkun, *Religion and the Racist Right*, 6.

3. Roy, *Apostles of Discord*, 92–93.

4. Ibid., 93.

5. See Abanes, *American Militias*, 161.

6. *$100 Billion Lien.*

7. Barkun, *Religion and the Racist Right*, 15.

8. Ibid., 47–52.

9. Roy, *Apostles of Discord*, 27–29.

10. Barkun, *Religion and the Racist Right*, 52–54.

11. Roy, *Apostles of Discord*, 59.

12. Barkun, *Religion and the Racist Right*, 68–70.

13. For current work on the militia see Abanes, *American Militias*.

14. Wistrich, *Hitler's Apocalypse*, 36.

15. Poliakov, *The Aryan Myth*, 199; Mosse, *Toward the Final Solution*, 39.

16. For a survey of "Early Myths of Origin" see Poliakov, *The Aryan Myth*, 13–122.

17. Ibid., 100.

18. Ibid., 260.

19. Mosse, *Toward the Final Solution*, 155.

20. Ibid., 160.

21. Ibid., 67.

22. Ibid., 162.

23. Wistrich, *Hitler's Apocalypse*, 93–97.

24. Poliakov, *The Aryan Myth*, 217.

25. Ibid., 237.

26. *In the Image of God*, 60; Hallimore, *God's Great Race*, 1, 3; Gentry, *Death Penalty*, 9–10; E. R. Fields, *Interracial Dating/Interracial Marriage: Right or Wrong?* Truth Tract #7 available from *The Truth at Last*, Marietta, Ga.; Hoskins, *Our Nordic Race*, 72.

27. See Michael D. Biddiss, *The Father of Racist Ideology: The Social and Political Thought of Count Gobineau* (New York: Weybright and Talley, 1970); Geoffrey G. Field, *Evangelist of Race: The Germanic Vision of Houston Stewart Chamberlain* (New York: Columbia University Press, 1981), 152.

28. Mosse, *Toward the Final Solution*, 52.

29. Poliakov, *The Aryan Myth*, 237.

30. George Mosse, *The Crisis of German Ideology: Intellectual Origins of the Third Reich* (New York: Universal Library, 1964), 91.

31. Poliakov, *The Aryan Myth*, 238.

32. Ibid., 307.

33. Fritz Stern, *The Politics of Cultural Despair: A Study in the Rise of the Germanic Ideology* (Berkeley: University of California Press, 1974), 63.

34. Mosse, *The Crisis of German Ideology*, 39.

35. Field, *Evangelist of Race*, 400.

36. Poliakov, *The Aryan Myth*, 319. See also Field, *Evangelist of Race*, 29.

37. Field, *Evangelist of Race*, 182.

38. See the extremist works in National Vanguard Book Catalog, 24; Hoskins, *Our Nordic Race*, 29.

39. Mosse, *The Crisis of German Ideology*, 102.

40. Poliakov, *The Aryan Myth*, 270.

41. Mosse, *Toward the Final Solution*, 110.

42. Ibid., 165.

43. Mosse, *The Crisis of German Ideology*, 170.

44. Mosse, *Toward the Final Solution*, 207.

45. Ibid., 209.

46. Lucy S. Dawidowicz, *The War against the Jews, 1933–1945* (New York: Holt, Rinehart & Winston, 1975), 58.

47. Mosse, *Toward the Final Solution*, 212.

48. Ibid., 212. (See also Wistrich, *Hitler's Apocalypse*, 83.)

49. Ibid., 209.

50. Ibid., 216.

51. Ibid., 218.

52. Wistrich, *Hitler's Apocalypse*, 176–77, 188.

53. Horsman, *Race and Manifest Destiny*, 219.

54. Julius Pratt, "The Origin of Manifest Destiny," *American Historical Review*, no. 32 (July 1927): 795–98, 796 (quotation).

55. Horsman, *Race and Manifest Destiny*, 90.

56. Ibid., 101.

57. Ibid., 36.

58. See Paul Boyer, *When Time Shall Be No More: Prophecy Belief in Modern American Culture* (Cambridge: Harvard University Press, 1992), 56–79. In this ethos the Mormon Church (the Church of Jesus Christ of Latter-Day Saints) arose. According to Mormon teachings, North America is to be the site of the regathering of the tribes of Israel.

59. Ernest Lee Tuveson, *Redeemer Nation: The Idea of America's Millennial Role* (Chicago: University of Chicago Press, 1968), 55.

60. Boyer, *When Time Shall Be No More*, 70.

61. Cherry, *God's New Israel*, 59. See also Boyer, *When Time Shall Be No More*, 71–73, 184.

62. Tuveson, *Redeemer Nation*, 77.

63. Ibid, 57.

64. Ibid, 82.

65. Horsman, *Race and Manifest Destiny*, 56, 61.

66. Tuveson, *Redeemer Nation*, 166.

67. Horsman, *Race and Manifest Destiny,* 197.
68. Ibid., 205.
69. Ibid., 211.
70. Ibid., 214.
71. Ibid., 215.

8. OPPOSING THE NEW RACIAL EXTREMISTS

1. Martin Luther King Jr., "Letter from Birmingham Jail," in *God's New Israel: Religious Interpretations of American Destiny,* ed. Cherry Conrad (Englewood Cliffs, N.J.: Prentice-Hall, 1971), 355.

2. Gayman, *Two Seeds,* 11. See also Hoskins, *Our Nordic Race,* 66; Goff, *America: Zion of God,* 62.

3. Allen, *None Dare Call It Conspiracy,* 35. Charles H. Barbee is quoted from *Southern Poverty Law Center Klanwatch Intelligence Report,* no. 84 (November 1996): 4.

4. See Craig Welch, "Three Guilty in Valley Bombings," *Spokane Spokesman-Review,* July 24, 1997, Internet edition at <http://www.VirtuallyNW.com>. A fourth man received a sentence of fifty-five years for his role in the bombing and robbery spree; the investigation is not yet closed at this writing. Craig Welch, "Buckshot Now Focal Point at Bomb Trail," *Spokane Spokesman-Review,* July 8, 1997, Internet edition; Craig Welch, "Barbee Denies Any Involvement," *Spokane Spokesman-Review,* July 15, 1997, Internet edition; "Spokane Suspects Connected to Identity Church," *Southern Poverty Law Center Klanwatch Intelligence Report,* no. 84 (November 1996): 4.

5. Slobodzian, "Guilty Plea in Bank Heists by Hate Group"; Pitcavage, "Aryan Nations Leader Enters Surprise Guilty Plea"; "Terrorists in the Name of God and Race," *Southern Poverty Law Center Klanwatch Intelligence Report,* no. 83 (August 1996): 1–5.

6. Bill Morlin, "The War Within: Working Independently but with a Common Goal, Rebels throughout the Nation Are Attempting to Disrupt and Overthrow the Government," *Spokane Spokesman Review,* Dec. 29, 1996. The prisoner is Walter Thody.

7. Lane, *Under This Sign,* 2.

8. Richard Kelly Hoskins, *Vigilantes of Christendom: The Story of the Phineas Priesthood* (Lynchburg, Va.: Virginia Publishing, 1990). The sin punished by Phineas is certainly not race mixing, but intermarriage that leads to the worship of *false gods.* The primary concern is stated clearly and early in Numbers 25: The daughters of Moab "invited the people to the sacrifice of *their gods,* and the people ate and bowed down to *their gods*" (25:2). In the meal the people communed with an idol, in this case Baal of Peor, a local manifestation of the Canaanite storm and fertility deity: "Thus Israel yoked itself to the Baal of Peor" (25:3). God's "anger was kindled" (25:3) against the idolatry even before the Midianite woman was among the Israelites. The defense of the worship of Yahweh and the seduction of foreign gods was tightly bound to the seduction of foreign women. Marriage led to cultic

sin and idolatry, especially when the other gods were believed to be concerned about fertility.

The primary concern, idolatry, is substantiated by Psalm 106:28–31 (see also Joshua 22:11–20, 1 Macc. 2:15–26). What is recalled in the psalm and connected to Phineas's namesake is the disobedience of a people who "attached themselves" to an alien divinity. Though the radical measures employed to preserve true worship violate our current laws and sensibilities, the issue for which Phineas fought and the context in which Phineas is remembered was idolatry, not racial hygiene.

9. As early as 1980, Aryan Nations' Butler was visited by one of Europe's most famous neo-Nazis, Manfred Kurt Roeder, who had been barred from his law practice in West Germany because of his terrorist activities. The two exchanged international contacts (Stern, *A Force Upon the Plain*, 242).

10. Emry, *Who Killed Christ?*, 31.

11. Hoskins, *Our Nordic Race*, 70.

12. A sampling of sites on the Internet dedicated to spreading Identity includes Scriptures for America (Laporte, Colo.), Storm Front (West Palm Beach, Fla.), Be Wise As Serpents (Hawaii), New Beginnings (Waynesville, N.C.), the Covenant Vision Ministry (Mount Druitt Village, Australia), Aryan Nations (Hayden Lake, Idaho), Kingdom Identity Ministries (Harrison, Ark.), Gospel Ministries (Boise, Idaho), Northwest Kinsmen Homepage (Tacoma, Wash.), Weisman Publications (Burnsville, Minn.), Posse Comitatus (Munsing, Mich.), God's Order Affirmed in Love (GOAL), Bible Restoration Ministries (Royal Oak, Mich.), Christian Defense League (Arabi, La.), and the Gospel Broadcasting Association (Houston, Tex.). Cross-pollination between groups is evident in that Identity sites offer links to militia, revisionist, sovereignty, Second Amendment, conspiracy, and Patriot sites. Some record labels distributing racial extremist music over the Internet include Resistance Records (Ontario, Canada, and Detroit, Mich.), Rock Nord (Germany), Sunwheel Records (Baton Rouge, La.), Tri-State Terror (Stroudsburg, Pa.), and Boot Boys Records (Hokksund, Norway). Targeting youth, these record outlets feature such bands as No Remorse, Nordic Thunder, Celtic Warrior, Extreme Hatred, and RAHOWA (an abbreviation for Racial Holy War). See Michael Janofsky, "Anti-Defamation League Warns of Web Hate Sites," *New York Times*, October 22, 1997.

13. Gayman, *Two Seeds*, 8–9.

14. Scott, *Kingdom Stories for Children*, 11, 24.

15. Ibid., 9, 47. Available from Kingdom Identity Ministries, Harrison, Ark.

16. For helpful discussion concerning the role of religion in public life see Stephen Carter, *The Culture of Disbelief: How American Law and Politics Trivialize Religious Devotion* (New York: Anchor Books, 1993); see 13, 8.

17. Martin Luther King Jr., "Letter from Birmingham Jail," as quoted in *God's New Israel*, 356.

18. Charles B. Cousar, *Galatians*, Interpretation (Louisville, Ky.: John Knox Press, 1982), 9.

19. Jürgen Moltmann, *The Church in the Power of the Spirit* (London: SCM Press, 1977), 343.

20. Considering the slavery question, Paul added to the direction given in 3:28 in his letter to Philemon concerning the return of the runaway slave Onesimus. Paul returned Onesimus to Philemon "no longer as a slave but more than a slave, a beloved brother [in Christ]" (Philem. 16). Paul was not simply after freedom from slavery, but freedom for a new relationship. He moved beyond freedom as autonomy to, in that case, brotherhood. In other places Paul might seem to condone slavery. But his admonishments to slaves must be seen in light of his lively expectation that the end of the age would come soon, or in Paul's own words, "in view of the impending crisis" (1 Cor. 7:26).

The issue of gender is analogous. Paul's statement in 3:28 is revolutionary. And yet at other places Paul gave the impression that males were to play a dominant role in the church and in life. He did not attack the problem of male dominance head-on. But again we need to remember the revolutionary leanings of 3:28 and the fact that, given the cultural and social conditions of Paul's day, the passages that seem to convey a conservative message were quite radical. Also, Paul mentioned working side by side with women on his missionary journeys, as partners in the gospel, not as subordinates.

21. Arthur C. Cochrane, *The Church's Confession under Hitler* (Philadelphia: Westminster Press, 1962), 205.

22. "The Declaration, Resolutions, and Motions Adopted by the Synod of Barmen, May 29–31, 1934" is reprinted in whole in *The Church's Confession under Hitler,* 237–47. The word "evangelical" is often used in the United States to designate a fairly recent movement in the Christian church called fundamentalism. Karl Barth, professor, theologian, and resister of the "German Christians" under Hitler, helps with how the word "evangelical" is used in this work: "What the word 'evangelical' will objectively designate is that theology which treats the God of the Gospel. . . . Such theology intends to apprehend, to understand, and to speak of the God of the Gospel, in the midst of the variety of all other theologies" (Karl Barth, *Evangelical Theology: An Introduction* [New York: Holt, Rinehart, and Winston, 1963], 5). In this light, not all so-called Protestant theology is evangelical, and there is evangelical theology in the Roman Catholic and Eastern Orthodox Churches.

23. Synod of Barmen, from Cochrane, *The Church's Confession under Hitler,* Section 2, 239; Section 2, 242; Section 5, 244.

24. Gunther Gassman, "Confession and Communion. Ecclesiological Implications of the Lutheran World Federation's 1977 Status Confessionis Statement," Lutheran World Federation Documentation no. 41, 195.

25. Cochrane, *The Church's Confession under Hitler,* 248–67, 211.

26. Ibid., 275.

27. Nils Alstrup Dahl, "The Doctrine of Justification: Its Social Function and Implications," in *Studies in Paul* (Minneapolis: Augsburg Fortress,

1977), 108. See also Markus Barth, "Jews and Gentiles: The Social Character of Justification in Paul," *Journal of Ecumenical Studies* 5 (1968): 241–67; Eberhard Jungel, *Death: The Riddle and the Mystery,* trans. Iain and Ute Nicol (Philadelphia: Westminster Press, 1974), 122–26.

28. Dietrich Bonhoeffer, *Life Together,* trans. John Doberstein (New York: Harper & Row, 1954), 21.

29. Jungel, *Death: The Riddle and the Mystery,* 125.

30. For a complete copy of the Memorandum see Appendix X, "Memorandum Submitted to Chancellor Hitler, June 4, 1936," in Cochrane, *The Church's Confession under Hitler,* 268–79.

31. Ibid., 208.

32. Ibid., 210.

33. Abraham Heschel, *The Prophets: An Introduction* (New York: Harper Torchbooks, 1962), 1:168, 191.

34. Cochrane, *The Church's Confession under Hitler,* 236–37.

35. Trachtenberg, *The Devil and the Jews,* 165.

36. Ibid., 44, 93. Statement by Roman Catholic theologian Johannes Eck.

37. "We Remember: A Reflection on the Shoah," *Commission for Religious Relations with the Jews,* Vatican City, March 16, 1998; "The Declaration of the Evangelical Lutheran Church in America to the Jewish Community," Church Council of the Evangelical Lutheran Church in America, April 18, 1994.

38. Becker, *The Denial of Death,* 178.

39. Bonhoeffer, *Life Together,* 86.

40. Gerhard O. Forde, *Theology Is for Proclamation* (Minneapolis: Fortress Press, 1990).

41. There are definite shortcomings to television as a tool to engage the public: (1) television loves a pretty, friendly face; (2) one can avoid questions asked and still get fifteen to twenty seconds of airtime by listening carefully and then repeating a desired message; (3) television has no memory, making it difficult and complicated to create an in-depth story; and (4) television loves conflict that makes a quick, easy story. These aspects explain in part why David Duke—whose racial extremist background is long, clear, and undeniable—could win a seat in the Louisiana House of Representatives. For a helpful discussion see Gary Esolen's "More Than a Pretty Face: David Duke's Use of Television as a Political Tool," in *The Emergence of David Duke,* 136–55.

42. For example, after explaining Identity's two-seed theory of the origins of humankind to a Washington State newspaper reporter, I was misquoted as stating that the Identity theory was that "white people are descendants of Abel." Abel, however, had no offspring because he was murdered by Cain (Gen. 4:8). The writer meant Seth, who was conceived by Eve through Adam after Abel's death.

43. John Taylor, "Church Rebukes Militia: Members of Noxon Methodist Church Speak Up," *Billings Gazette,* June 25, 1995, 6C.

44. Jerry Walters, "Local Pastor Explains 'Freemen' Movement," *Roundup Record Tribune,* June 14 (p. 2), June 21 (p. 2), June 28 (p. 2), 1995.

45. Niebuhr, *Children of Light and Children of Darkness,* 132.

46. Ibid., 133, 130.

47. Ibid., 137–38.

48. Heschel, *The Prophets,* 2:64.

49. "Letter from Birmingham Jail," in *God's New Israel,* 352.

50. Senator Max Baucus, "The Militias and Freemen in Montana," statement to the Senate Subcommittee on Terrorism, Technology and Government Information, Washington, D.C., June 15, 1995.

51. Niebuhr, *Children of Light and Children of Darkness,* 124.

52. Louis Sahagun, "A Wave of Distrust in the West," *Billings Gazette,* February 3, 1995, 1A.

53. Kathleen McLaughlin, "Bill Targets Threats of 'Freemen,'" *Billings Gazette,* March 4, 1995, 1A.

INDEX

abortion, 42, 77
Adam, 3, 11–15, 17–19, 30, 34, 121
n. 17; Adamic race, 3, 19–21,
31, 33, 37–38, 42, 106; future
of seed of Adam, 32–33; seed
of Adam, 1, 18–19, 21, 23, 26,
31–32, 34–38, 42
Ahlwart, Hermann, 87
America, as promised land. *See*
United States
America: Zion of God (Goff), 31, 64
American Institute of Theology, 66
American Revolution, 89, 90
America's Promise Ministries, 95
anti-Semitism, 15; Arab, 35, 49, 84;
Reformation, 56–61. *See also*
Nazis
apocalypse, 9, 43, 45, 61, 83, 90,
94; racial apocalypse, 32–33.
See also war
Aryan Nations, 2, 4, 12, 27, 54,
70–72, 82, 95
Aryan Republican Army, 55, 69,
95
Aryans, 6–7, 23, 43, 45, 95, 103;
Aryan Paragraph, 102; christol-
ogy, 81; cradle of Aryan race,
19–20, 83; and creation, 12–13;
and the future, 32–33; and

Jesus, 27; and Nazism 82–85,
88; and politics, 74. *See also*
Nazis

baptism, 16, 59, 100
Barmen Declaration, 102–6. *See
also* Confessing Church in Nazi
Germany
Barth, Karl, 102, 141 n. 22
Beach, Henry "Mike," 4, 82
Beam, Louis, 69
Bellamy, Joseph, 91
Benton, Thomas Hart, 90
black helicopters, 43, 130 n. 51
Bonhoeffer, Dietrich, 102–3, 109
Branch Davidians, 9, 53, 67, 82
British Israelism, 90, 96; mutation
to Identity, 81–82; and racial
salvation history, 78–80; in
United States, 80–81
Brothers, Richard, 79
Butler, Richard, 4, 12, 72, 82

Calhoun, John C., 92
Cameron, William J., 81
Canaanites. *See* seed of the ser-
pent, in promised land
Caucasians, 7, 10, 13, 24, 91–92,
110

ABOUT THE AUTHOR

Jerome Walters is a pastor in Washington State. He has been interviewed by major television and radio programs, including ABC's World News Tonight, A&E's The Road to Rapture, CBS Evening News, CNN's Talk Back Live, NBC's Evening News, National Public Radio, and UPI Radio News Service. He has lectured across the United States.